Preaching *with* All Ages

Preaching *with* All Ages

Twelve ways to grow your skills and your confidence

Ally Barrett

CANTERBURY
PRESS

Norwich

First published in 2019 by the Canterbury Press Norwich
Editorial office
3rd Floor, Invicta House
108–114 Golden Lane
London EC1Y 0TG, UK
www.canterburypress.co.uk

Canterbury Press is an imprint of Hymns Ancient & Modern Ltd
(a registered charity)

Hymns Ancient & Modern® is a registered trademark of
Hymns Ancient & Modern Ltd
13A Hellesdon Park Road, Norwich,
Norfolk NR6 5DR, UK

British Library Cataloguing in Publication data

A catalogue record for this book is available
from the British Library

978 1 78622 171 1

Typeset by Regent Typesetting
Printed and bound in Great Britain by
CPI Group (UK) Ltd

Contents

This book is dedicated to Sam, Joanna and Dan, without whom nothing would have been possible.

Acknowledgements

There are so many people to thank: first, Peter Moger, my training incumbent, who repeatedly pushed me off the all-age preaching cliff until I learned to fly, and the congregations who were patient with me along the way; and my students, who have put up with me trying things out on them over the past several years, and given me much-needed criticism as well as affirmation.

Thank you to the many colleagues who have shared their own experiences of all-age preaching with me so generously, who have helped shape my thinking and had the honesty to tell me when I am wrong – I am hugely grateful for their insights and wisdom, and all remaining inadequacies and errors are very much my own. Special thanks are due to those who allowed me to use their own stories and ideas in this book.

I would like to thank Christine, Mary, Hannah, Joanne and their colleagues who believed that this book was a good idea and made it happen. I'm incredibly grateful to the many friends who were willing to read draft versions and offer me helpful feedback.

Finally, I would like to thank my family: my parents, who first taught me to believe that 'someone has to do it'; my husband Sam, who taught me the value of critical thinking and perseverance; and my children, Joanna and Dan, who never stopped asking questions and in so many ways helped me to discover more of the love and mystery of God.

Encountering God

> 'Did you know that God is invisible? That means we can't see God. And did you also know that when we become invisible we'll be able to see God then?'

My son was four years old when he explained this to me, expressing an encounter with the divine that is as profound as it is simple. It prompted me to pay closer attention to what children might be able to offer to the whole Body of Christ as we encounter God together in worship and in preaching. Without the witness of children, the Church's encounter with God is impoverished.

As it is, there are many members, yet one body. The eye cannot say to the hand, 'I have no need of you', nor again the head to the feet, 'I have no need of you.' On the contrary, the members of the body that seem to be weaker are indispensable ... If one member suffers, all suffer together with it; if one member is honoured, all rejoice together with it. *(1 Corinthians 12.20–22, 26)*

Introduction

Worshipping and preaching with all ages

This book is about preaching with all ages.

It's not a book of ready-made all-age talks; there are already plenty of good books that offer this. Rather, it's about understanding how all-age preaching is shaped by, and shapes, its context, embodying a culture in which everyone is valued. It's also about how we can learn from our experience, growing in confidence as we open up God's word afresh with every generation. [1]

- **Preaching** *to* a congregation reminds us that as preachers we carry a degree of authority bestowed by the Church and its people to share God's good news.
- **Preaching** *for* a congregation reminds us that sharing this wisdom must take into account the needs of the whole people of God.
- **Preaching** *with* a congregation facilitates an encounter with God, drawing on everyone's diverse experiences and gifts to discern God's purposes together.

Preaching *to* and preaching *for* are well understood as essential to all forms of preaching, so one of the main purposes of this book is to explore what the idea of preaching *with* adds to our understanding, and what it looks like in real life, including:

---

1 This idea appears in the Church of England's liturgies for the Admission and Licensing of Readers, and for the licensing of clergy.

- Making room for questions, ideas, doubts and surprises.
- Attending to people's hopes and fears, gifts and needs.
- Opening ourselves to the Holy Spirit as we explore the riches of God's word.
- Creating a hospitable space in which all people can contribute and be heard.
- Sharing some of our own power by empowering others.
- Discovering our ability to make connections and draw out fruitful themes.
- Setting preaching in the context of worship, church life, community and God's world.
- Growing in confidence as we learn to trust God, the congregation and ourselves.

Worshipping together

Preaching isn't a stand-alone activity: it's part of worship. What does it mean to worship together? All-age worship – now more commonly called 'intergenerational worship' – is on the in-  crease. Many denominations provide liturgical material for inter-generational congregations, in most local churches at least some services have children and adults worshipping, learning and growing together. Yet in some places it still feels counter-cultural, so it's worth reminding ourselves why it matters – and the variety of motivations that may lie behind worshipping together.

'All-age worship is normal'

- Church is one of the few contexts in western culture where all ages regularly gather.
- Church can be an opportunity for families to do something together.
- If we assume that worshipping together is normal, any segregation (by age or other factors) has to be for a good reason and for everyone's benefit.

'All who believed were together and had all things in common ... Day by day, as they spent much time together in the temple, they broke bread at home and ate their food with glad and generous hearts, praising God and having the goodwill of all the people.' (Acts 2.44–46)

- Worshipping together helps us learn about one another's gifts and needs, and balance these so that everyone can flourish within the Body of Christ in all its diversity.

'All-age worship builds community'

- When all ages worship and open up the word of God together we learn from one another.
- Worshipping and learning *together* can help dispel the idea that worship is an adult activity while learning is for children.[2]

'We started a monthly all-age service, and encouraged the children to take leadership roles, such as serving or playing in the band, leading the prayers and reading, or helping on the sound desk.'

- Intergenerational activities (including worship) foster mutual support on the journey of faith.

---

2 For a fuller exploration of this, see Stephen Burns, *Worship in Context: Liturgical Theology, Children and the City*, London: Epworth Press, 2006, p. 150.

- Worshipping together helps children to 'take their place within the life and worship of Christ's Church',[3] so that when they grow out of Sunday school they don't grow out of church.

'All-age worship is missional'

- Intergenerational worship can attract families to church – they can come as they are.
- Building links with local schools and nurseries, and good follow-up after baptisms, can grow all-age congregations.
- Churches that still have a 'parade' service that includes children's uniformed organizations can involve those children and leaders in planning the worship.[4]
- We can connect with the secular calendar as well as the church calendar, focusing on issues and themes that resonate with our community.
- We might need to review how we worship to ensure that services are accessible to those who aren't used to church.

'Go … and make disciples of all nations, baptizing them in the name of the Father and of the Son and of the Holy Spirit.'
(Matthew 28.19)

---

3 From the baptism service in *Common Worship: Initiation*, London: Church House Publishing, 2005.

4 In most places church parade numbers are falling, and it can also be hard to reach whole families this way, as children often attend with a group leader rather than with a parent, but where groups are active and committed you may reach children this way who would never otherwise be in church.

'All-age worship is practical'

- Worshipping with all ages together can be a practical response to a lack of resources, personnel or venue for children's groups.
- The service may not be very different from what would have been designed for an adult congregation – children simply join in.
- Children may have parallel activities in the pews or a children's corner – these can be related to what's going on in the worship.[5]
- Children are warmly welcomed, sharing in the ordinary life of a congregation, helping give out hymn books, lighting candles, ringing the bell, and so on – they are formed in the faith by 'osmosis' and by the example of the adults around them.

> 'We used to just have a corner at the back with some old toys in it, then we introduced more art materials, and gradually replaced the old toys with ones that encouraged the children's participation, such as toy communion sets, colouring book versions of the service sheet, and teddies that you could dress to look like the vicar.'

No two all-age congregations are the same. Churches that would love to have a children's group may end up worshipping together due to lack of resources, while churches that desperately want to worship intergenerationally may struggle to make it work for everyone. The worship may be fully intergenerational or may (deliberately or accidentally) prioritize one age group over another – it's well worth looking critically at our worship to see if this is happening. There may always be the same children there, or it may vary from week to week – and sometimes there may not be any children there at all.

There's an important principle here, which may help you work out how to approach the task of preaching with all ages.

---

5 Including liturgy boxes: see http://www.spiritualchild.co.uk/liturgyboxes. html for ideas of what to include in these.

> 'If your talk doesn't work without the children, it's not all-age.'
> *Mary Hawes, the Church of England's National Adviser*
> *for Children and Youth*

All-age preachers

All-age preaching is not the same as preaching for children. It is preaching that genuinely seeks to open up the word of God to a congregation in which there may be any combination of toddlers and teenagers, long-retired elderly and energetic 80-year-olds, working and non-working adults with or without partners and children, in such a way that those diverse people can encounter God together. No wonder preaching with all ages can feel so daunting.

If you find it hard, remember this: for many people – including young families – it's really hard just getting to church. By making it to the service, they've already gone the extra mile. If we have children in church, it's because someone in their life believes it's worth them being there. Preaching and planning worship that takes their needs and gifts into account really matters: it communicates how glad we are that they have come, and through it we can offer to the whole diverse Body of Christ an experience of intergenerational community that perhaps only the Church can provide.

My own denomination, the Church of England, places high value on preaching and is quite guarded about who may preach regularly. It expects its preachers to have the capacity to understand and interpret scripture, theological tradition and human experience, and to integrate these in such a way that the gospel is proclaimed afresh in every generation, nourishing God's people in their journey of life and faith and speaking prophetically into the complexity of the contemporary world.

In some churches, preaching with all ages is described as 'giving a talk', perhaps to differentiate it from what that church considers to be 'proper' preaching, and to open it up to those who might not otherwise be authorized to preach. This book aims to raise the profile of preaching with all ages – it is just as important as any other kind of preaching, and deserves to be well resourced and well respected.

Whatever your context, you're probably reading this book because you're already involved in all-age preaching and want to increase your confidence, or because your church is about to try this for the first time or develop it in a new direction. Here are some of the most common concerns that this book tries to help with – maybe some of these resonate with you.

'But all-age preaching is scary'

Preaching an all-age sermon may take you well outside your comfort zone. All-age preaching is often delegated to people who may not feel qualified, resourced or called to do it. But the Bible is full of stories of people whom God called out of their comfort zone: Abraham, Moses, David, Mary, Peter … We know their stories because they rose to the challenge and, with God's help, faced their fears. Maybe this is the leap of faith that God is asking of you, if you can 'get comfortable with being uncomfortable'.[6]

'I don't have what it takes'

Realizing that preaching with all ages is challenging is a sign that you're taking it seriously and are motivated to do it well. Make the

---

6 See Robert Poynton, *Do Improvise,* London: The Do Book Company, 2013, p. 94.

most of any resources or training you're offered, to help build up your skills and confidence, and use this book to help you reflect on your own practice so that you are learning and growing as an all-age preacher. Nobody gets it right all the time. Learning from difficult experiences goes hand in hand with building a real relationship with those among whom we preach, and that can only be a good thing.

'All-age ministry doesn't connect with the rest of church life'

Sometimes all-age services have a distinct congregation, and key players in the life of the church may even stay away, thinking that all-age worship is 'not their thing'. For all sorts of reasons there may not be great communication between the people who are preaching with all ages and the church's leadership. All-age preaching can all too easily become a stand-alone, as well as an under-resourced, activity, and it can take time and persistence to create a culture in which all-age and intergenerational activity, including worship and preaching, is seen as intrinsic to the church's life and identity. It may be part of your calling as an all-age preacher to contribute to this process of greater integration.

'I'll have to change the way I do things'

If you're used to preaching from a script, it can be hard to let go of that sense of control. Over time we can become more confident, learning to embrace the unexpected. We may even find that the experience of preaching with

all ages is changing us, making us more open, more trusting, more imaginative. Change can be scary, but it doesn't have to be bad.

How this book works

This book is not a traditional 'how to' guide, nor is it a collection of instructions to be repeated word for word and action for action. The heart of the book is a collection of 12 reflections, each one narrating one of my own experiences of preaching with all ages and drawing from it some principles, values and questions that I hope will be helpful. I am using my own experiences not because I am upholding them as the best or the only models for all-age preaching, but because only through using my own experiences can I access and draw out and share as much learning as possible.

At the end of each reflection is a 'follow-up' box indicating which of the remaining chapters of the book explore the emerging themes in more detail. These chapters each take a significant aspect of preaching with all ages and expand on it through a combination of theory and additional examples to build up a picture of what the ideas look like in real life.

I hope that this book will encourage you to undertake your own process of reflection-on-practice, as I have done in writing it. Use the ideas, but make them your own, and subject them to your own processes of discernment – you are *you*, not me, nobody knows your context like you do, and *you* are the one called to preach with your congregation. Use the questions I have suggested at various points in your own thinking and in conversation with your fellow ministers to generate wisdom in and for your own context, drawing on the gifts and experience that are around you and within you.

Try completing the exercise on the following page.

When I think about preaching with all ages:

I am thankful for:

I am hopeful about:

I worry about:

What underlying values, hopes and fears are at the heart of this, for you and for your church?

Are there particular circumstances or past history in your context or in your own life that might affect how you approach preaching with all ages?

Bring your hopes and fears to God – initially just by yourself, then if you can, seek prayerful support and encouragement from your church leadership or ministry team.

1

Reflecting on the resurrection

The evening of Holy Saturday I was at home, procrastinating about my Easter all-age talk for the next morning. I found myself on Twitter, which was full of 'Happy Easter' and 'Alleluia' tweets from people returning from early Easter Vigils. My church didn't hold an Easter Vigil, so I kept wanting to reply 'Spoiler-alert! We haven't had our resurrection yet!' It reminded me, too, that in the morning I would effectively be 'having the resurrection' three times – one for each service I was taking. As I tried to work out why this niggled, I found myself with an idea for my talk for the morning.

The Gospel reading for the day was John 20.1–18: Mary in the garden, 'while it was still dark'.

I began by holding up a hollow chocolate egg, while I talked about the darkness of the morning and the darkness inside the tomb.

'Inside it's dark. It's like Good Friday.

'But when the resurrection happened, Jesus burst out of the tomb – in one of the other Gospels there's even an earthquake! Good Friday is smashed once and for all, and new life is set free.'

At this point I dramatically smashed the egg into a bowl.

'But the trouble was, nobody witnessed it! In the story with the earthquake, the soldiers fainted and missed it, and the next thing we know, it's the women arriving at the tomb still expecting to find a body, and instead finding it empty. The actual moment of the resurrection happened in private. All that resurrection joy and nobody to share it.'

At this point I held up another chocolate egg.

'There in the garden, the resurrection had already happened, but Mary was trapped in her own Good Friday – her grief and sadness kept her feeling like she was still in the dark.

'And I think we can tell the exact moment when the resurrection happened for Mary – it's when Jesus calls her name, she recognizes him and realizes he is alive. Suddenly grief is turned to joy. Mary's Good Friday is smashed once and for all, the new life is set free in her.'

At this point I smashed the second egg and handed round the bowl.

'The resurrection was a real moment – a life-changing, life-bringing moment in the history of the world. No going back. But it becomes real for us at different times and in different situations.'

At this point we carried on with the Easter stories, giving ourselves some 'spoilers' as to what we'd be hearing in church over the next few weeks. In each case, Jesus' friends get their own moment when the resurrection becomes real for them. I got the congregation to remind each other of the stories, focusing particularly on the moment of transformation. Each time we identified the 'resurrection moment' we smashed and shared another egg.

- For the disciples in the upper room, it's when Jesus walks through the locked door of their fear and breathes his peace on them. The resurrection feels like fear turning to peace.

- For Thomas, it's a week later: Jesus comes specially to find him and lets him touch his wounds and see his scars. The resurrection feels like doubt turning to faith.
- For the disciples at Emmaus it's the moment when Jesus breaks the bread. For them the resurrection feels like confusion turning to confidence.
- For Peter it's when Jesus gives him three opportunities to say 'I love you', to make up for the three times Peter denied him. The resurrection looks like guilt turning to forgiveness.

None of these stories takes place at the very moment of the resurrection, they are all afterwards – perhaps only by minutes for Mary, but for the others it's hours, maybe days or weeks before the resurrection becomes real for them.

This is still happening now. The resurrection was a historical moment, but the very fact that nobody was there to see it at the time means that each time we meet with the risen Jesus today is just as important as when Mary and  the Disciples met him. We did not miss out by living almost two thousand years after the event, because it is fresh every Easter, every Sunday, potentially every moment of every day. Whenever we realize that Christ has spoken into our grief, or walked through the locked door of our fear, or touched our doubt into faith, or our guilt into forgiveness …

Reflecting back on this, I notice a few things.

What started as an odd and slightly irritating moment for me gained theological meaning when I paused to reflect on it – asking 'Why do I feel this?' is always a worthwhile question. I love the Easter

Vigil service with all its drama and beauty, so there was a part of me that always felt as if I was missing out on the 'real thing'. Reflecting on the Easter stories this way was, perhaps, something that I needed to hear, and this very much shaped my planning.

But was it what others needed to hear? Did this talk enable the congregation (of all ages) to encounter God? The central idea that the resurrection, though historical and universal, is also fresh and personal did seem to be something that would resonate with people. Hopefully, focusing on the human, emotional stories of resurrection would enable people to connect their own journey of faith with scripture. This is something I've since tried on other occasions such as Christmas.

My choice of symbol (the chocolate egg) worked well: it was readily available and appealing, and could function on a number of levels:

- Planning a sermon late in the day (even after thinking about it for weeks) is a besetting sin of mine. Being limited to what I have to hand because I've left things late can also be liberating: instead of planning something complicated, I used what I already had – something that would be common to the whole congregation. I hoped people would remember what we'd talked about as they ate their own chocolate eggs later. Sometimes our last-minute-ness can also leave room for us to work with what God is providing.
- Something interactive, sensory and fun can help to capture attention, and encourage people's imagination. Holding the egg while reflecting on Mary's 'Good Friday' connected it with the emotional and spiritual layers of the story: smashing the egg then worked at a physical level to express a moment of transformation, a point of no return. For each story the eggs helped us identify and articulate this moment, as if we had acted it out.
- While I was speaking, I noticed some of the younger children starting to act out the emotional journey, curling in on themselves when I talked about sadness, and uncurling when it turned to joy. I began to reflect this slightly in my own body language.

- Chocolate is almost, but not quite, universally enjoyed. I had included 'free from' eggs in case of allergies or special diets. This is good practice in terms of safety and, in this case, it helped the medium and message to match one another: if the gospel message is 'the resurrection is for everyone' then we need to ensure that nobody is excluded because of the medium we have chosen.[1]
- The chocolate was broken to be shared – the process of sharing something good echoes the sharing of the good news by the characters in the stories. We deliberately didn't share the first broken egg until it had been joined by Mary's egg – the good news of the resurrection was first hers to be shared.

When I was delivering this talk it felt interactive, but I didn't give as much space for conversation or open questions as I might normally do; participation was through engagement with the stories, identifying the 'resurrection moments', and sharing in the sensory experience of the chocolate. The repeating structure of the stories and actions made it relatively straightforward to facilitate. If I had wanted to make it more fully participatory, I could have invited members of the congregation to smash some of the eggs, if a particular part of the narrative resonated with them, perhaps even inviting them to share something of their own story. This is not something I would do lightly – symbolic actions can be powerful and make people more vulnerable than they might want to be in the context of an all-age service.

I had wondered whether the activity was too formulaic, though on reflection it felt like an appropriate – almost liturgical – use of repetition.

I worried afterwards whether focusing on the emotional journeys and moments of transformation might have failed to leave room for those in the congregation whose own Good Friday was real and ongoing, and for whom believing that Jesus was risen from the dead did not change how they experienced the reality of their life circum-

---

1 In some traditions it's the custom to fast before receiving communion. In this case, it might be worth waiting to distribute the chocolate just before the final blessing.

stances. Easter is an occasion of real joy. It is the triumph of life over death, light over darkness, love over hatred. But the world we live in doesn't always feel as if life, light and love have won. As preachers we don't always know what's going on for people, but being willing to share experiences of brokenness in preaching can reassure people that they are not as alone in their suffering as they thought.

This concern makes a good case for the preacher working alongside those leading other aspects of the service, such as the prayers, which could have responded to pastoral need.

> Lord Jesus,
> When life makes us weep,
> meet us where we are and call us by name.
> When we are afraid,
> meet us where we are and give us your peace in our hearts.
> When we are confused and full of doubt,
> meet us where we are and help us believe.
> When we are lost and ashamed,
> meet us where we are, remind us of your love for us,
> and teach us to love you and one another more and more.

You can follow up some of these themes in:

Chapter 2: Engaging through theological reflection
Chapter 4: Engaging through the senses
Chapter 6: Engaging in different ways
Chapter 12: Medium and message, process and product
Chapter 20: Engaging with human experience.

2

Engaging through theological reflection

Theological reflection is often included in the curriculum for ministers-in-training, particularly in relation to pastoral care – it's incredibly useful for preaching, too, and this chapter sets out a way of using it as we preach with all ages.[1]

In theological reflection, we pay attention to the interaction between ourselves, a particular context or situation and the Christian tradition (including scripture), because doing so can help us discern how to respond to particular situations, to connect our values with our practice, and to learn and grow more generally as human beings, disciples and ministers. The trajectory is always towards transformation – of ourselves, of others, and ultimately of the world around us. Theological reflection is a *critical*, *constructive*, *integrative* and *prayerful* process:

---

1 *The Art of Theological Reflection*, by Patricia O'Connell Killen and John de Beer (New York: Crossroad, 1994), explores how theological reflection can be used in a variety of ways in ministry. It is well worth reading.

It is *critical*	It is *constructive*	It is *integrative*	It is *prayerful*
It asks tough questions, not accepting everything at face value, but scratching beneath the surface to seek truth and wisdom.	It seeks healing, reconciliation and the building up of the Body of Christ.	It brings together different perspectives, valuing what is learned from experience as well as from theological tradition.	It treats experience, as well as theology, as 'holy ground', and seeks to discern the purposes of God.

We can draw on theological reflection in relation to preaching with all ages at four stages:

1 We can use it in the **planning** of our talk to help us think holistic-ally, imaginatively and accountably.
2 We can use it during the **delivery** of our talk to help us respond 'on the hoof' to changing circumstances, without losing the theo-logical and pastoral thread.
3 We can use it **after the event** to help us reflect on and learn from an experience of preaching.
4 Finally, it can help with our overall **learning and growth** as a minister as we learn how preaching with all ages works and what underlying values are shaping it, as well as learning more about our context, the people among whom we minister, and ourselves.

1 Planning – discerning the gospel in the gospel

Responding to the call to proclaim the faith 'afresh in every genera-tion'[2] or indeed to 'proclaim the gospel in word and deed' and 'preach the word in season and out of season',[3] we are faced with the chal-lenge of working out what that gospel is. What is God's good news for God's people in God's world today?

To discern the gospel in the gospel we must enable a conversation between all the perspectives on the day's scripture. It is this that enables us to reach a place of learning and growing not only for ourselves but for the congregation among whom the talk will be delivered. This approach is described as 'ecological', because it sees scripture not as an object in isolation but as the living word of God interacting creatively with everything in its complex environment. Each perspective sheds a light or casts a shadow on the word, while the word itself reveals something profound about the perspective from which we approach it.

1 The scriptural text or texts

This might be determined by a lectionary or chosen locally – we may have some choice about which of the readings for the day we want to focus on. What factors affect our choices?

How do we access the scripture for ourselves and share it with the congregation? Every translation, every proclamation of the gospel is an act of interpretation, as we make decisions about what themes to

---

2 www.churchofengland.org/prayer-and-worship/worship-texts-and-resources/common-worship/ministry/declaration-assent.

3 www.churchofengland.org/prayer-and-worship/worship-texts-and-resources/common-worship/ministry/common-worship-ordination-services.

bring out, which details are essential. How does this reading relate to the overarching witness of scripture?

2 The liturgical context: season, occasion and the act of worship

This includes the time of year, and the key themes associated with it, as well as any seasonal actions or objects that we need to engage with (such as Advent wreaths, crib scenes etc.). The season or occasion might also affect the 'tone' of our preaching, too.

Is the service eucharistic? This may be the natural focus, and the preaching may point to it. If not, is the talk itself required to be the focal point of the service?

Whether or not we are preaching and planning/leading the whole service, we may be able to work with others to integrate the talk into the worship as a whole, including prayers, hymns and songs.

3 Ministry and mission priorities

What are the prevailing themes and priorities that are shaping church life at the moment, globally, nationally, denominationally or locally? Are there key priorities that might affect the way that we unpack the scripture? Are there significant things happening in the life of our church that would benefit from being integrated prayerfully into preaching?

4 Contemporary issues: global, national and local

What is going on in the world, the nation and the local community? What will people have been talking about this week, or seen on the news? Will people of different ages or different socio-economic groups or living in different areas all be concerned about the same issues? Is anyone in our congregation personally affected by these wider issues? And how does all this affect how you read and hear the day's scripture?

5 The particular congregation: its diversity, needs, gifts and concerns

We preach to, for and with a particular group of people. Who are they? What diversity is there in terms of age, gender, socio-economic background, levels of literacy or education? What frames of reference or common experiences have shaped your community and your congregation over time? Are there any pastoral issues for individuals, families or the church as a whole that might affect how we preach, which themes we explore, and how we situate our talk in the wider pastoral context of our church's ministry? Remember, you are preaching with all ages, not just with the children in mind.

6 The preacher: experiences, knowledge and perspectives

Our own well-being, confidence, and concerns will shape how we approach our preaching. As Nadia Bolz-Weber puts it, we need to be able to preach from our scars – self-awareness is key.

What is occupying our mind and heart that might affect how we read the scripture? What does it mean to us, and is this meaning likely to be helpful for others? Will our previous experience with this story or passage help us this time?

7 Theological tradition: themes, images and wisdom

When we dwell with the scripture for a while, what images or ideas emerge for us? Where else have we encountered those ideas in scripture and in theological tradition? Where do we find them in liturgy, in church architecture, art or songs and hymns? How might they resonate with the congregation?

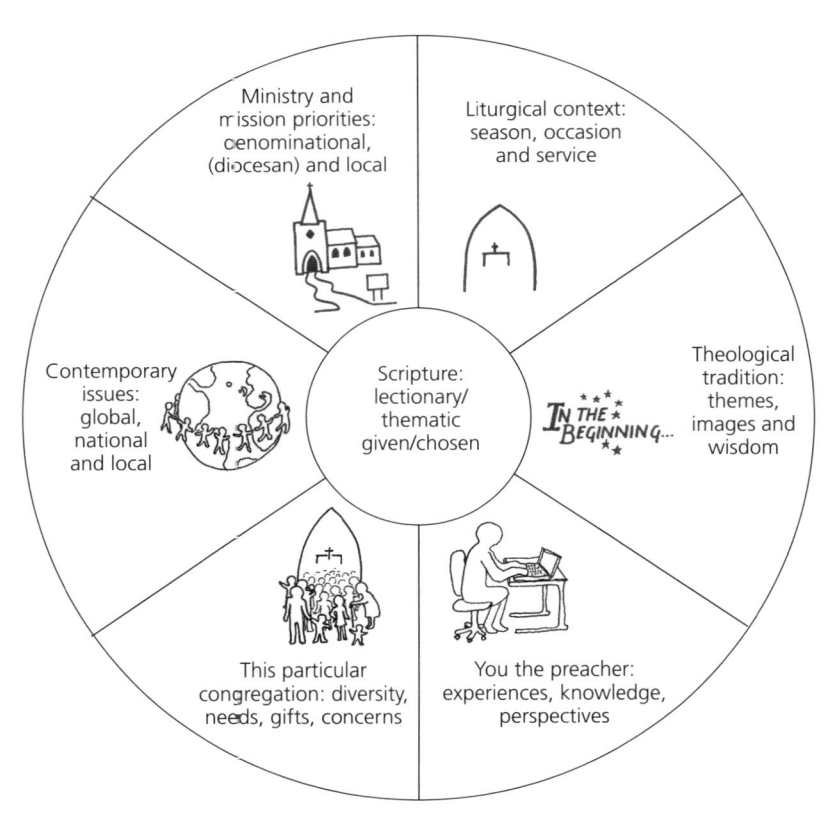

Our task as preachers is, in the power of the Holy Spirit, to help a congregation discern what the transformative 'good news' in this *text* is for these *people* in this *place*, in this local, national and global *context*, in this *service*, on this *day*, given that *we* are the ones who are preaching. The heart of the good news is unchanging, but it is an infinitely multifaceted jewel on which context shines a light, illuminating something slightly different every time – so if one parameter changes, it can really affect what we discern to be God's word for that day. The specific good news may be different for different people in the congregation – and our preaching can give them space to find that out.

You may also find the Godly Play 'wondering' questions helpful in this process:[4]

- I wonder which part [of the story] you like best?
- I wonder which part is the most important?
- I wonder which part is most about you?
- I wonder which part(s) could be left out and still have all that we need?

And then at the end:

- I wonder what work you will do today? (This invites a response beyond the act of worship.)

> 'I think I preach best in an all-age context when I think less about the message I want to convey, and more about the area of "wondering" that I want to open up for/with people. I think a lot more these days about questions than I do about answers.'
>
> *Ruth Harley*

---

4 Godly Play is one of several variations of the Montessori approach to Religious Education, as explained on the UK Godly Play website: www.godlyplay.uk/. For a fuller reflection on 'The Art of Wondering', see https://www.godlyplay.uk/wp-content/uploads/2013/05/The-Art-of-Wondering.pdf.

Preaching is the ultimate challenge of balancing responsiveness to the context and rootedness in the faith. Preaching with all ages is the most challenging of all since it fully embraces the variables within the congregation and within the form and delivery approaches available, and the added possibilities that real interactivity can bring.

Try out this process on a real talk. You may find it helpful to draw out your thinking on a big piece of paper, as a mind map (see opposite).

1 Read through your reading, noting any feelings that arise. When are you curious, or confused, comforted, or irritated? Try reading it in your head, and then aloud. Do you notice anything different?

2 Write down or highlight any words, phrases, images or themes that jump out at you.

3 For each of these, write down whatever springs to mind that connects with it – that might be in theology, in your own ordinary life experience, elsewhere in scripture, etc.

4 If anything you have written down so far looks fruitful, repeat the process with those items and see where they lead, connecting things with each other if you can.

5 Look at what you have produced so far, checking back over the ecological 'gospel in the gospel' approach to see if there's a perspective you've overlooked.

6 Does one theme or message seem to be emerging more than the others? Focus on this and think about how you might help your congregation unpack it, using ideas later in this book to help you think about the 'how'.

7 If you get stuck, share where you've got to with a friend or colleague, or with a child if you have one handy, and see what resonates with them.

Mind mapping

Here's a simple mind map, based on Luke 2.22–40, for a service that includes a baptism. See how some of the ideas connect with others, and especially with the baptism. In this case, we might want to look at using some of the words, symbols and actions in the baptism service during the talk – we might even think about spreading the talk out through the service rather than having it all at once.

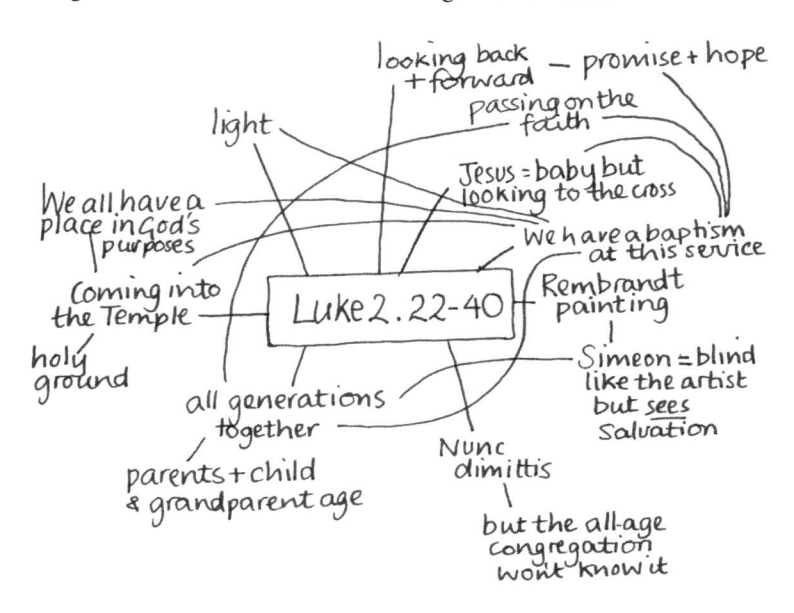

2 Delivery – the act of preaching

The same basic principles that we use to help us plan can also help us deliver what we planned – in fact, this must be so, since the particular congregation with which we are preaching is one of the parameters we were thinking about as we planned, and in the actual service we have the real thing with us. Other people that we invite into the process will always bring insights and perspectives that we've not thought of, and that's a gift. As the nominated preacher, it is our responsibility to facilitate what is, at heart, a communal theological reflection to which everyone is welcome to contribute. This approach to preaching with all ages may even encourage a broader change in ministry towards an ethos of openness.

This is one of the things that many people find most scary about preaching with all ages: the idea that we may have to field random contributions from the floor, be expected to weave them seamlessly into our script and still arrive at our intended destination on time. This is also why it can be so hard to use other people's talks: when we use someone else's script, we're less likely to be secure about what we're doing, and unexpected contributions will be hard to accommodate.

The approach I've set out here helps because it allows us to get to know the terrain, theologically and pastorally speaking: in discerning the 'gospel in the gospel' we will have sifted through a range of interpretations and ideas, some of which may well come up again as we invite others to contribute. This means that we are well placed to help the congregation explore, as we have done. We'll be more alert to interesting detours and potential danger areas, and hopefully have some ideas of what we might do if the congregation start to head down a road that could get tricky (pastorally or theologically). There is more about all this in Chapter 10.

The *process* and *attitude* of theological reflection can, over time, help us become open to the unexpected, more nimble in accommodating new ideas and insights and differences in perspective; it can also train us in becoming attentive to what God is doing and saying in and through others, and to the movement of the Holy Spirit through a community of faith.

> 'It is just as valid, and far more effective, to act yourself into a new way of thinking, than trying to think yourself into a new way of acting.'
>
> *Robert Poynton*[5]

---

5 Robert Poynton, *Do Improvise*, London: The Do Book Company, 2013.

In this, preaching with all ages is a little like jazz improvisation:

- A jazz musician needs to know the tune and the chords well, so they can dare to improvise and be sure they'll arrive back at the right place. For preachers, this means being rooted in the faith so that we can dare to ask open questions and explore.
- A jazz musician pays quality attention to what their fellow players are doing so that they can respond to one another's playing as a gift.
- A jazz musician practises scales and figurations so that they're at their fingertips when they need them. For preachers, this means turning words and phrases, images and actions over in our minds, regularly having informal conversations about God, faith and life, so that these are the things that are 'at our fingertips' when we need them in preaching.

By following this approach to our planning, we build up a resource bank of images, stories, feelings, actions, texts and ideas that can be drawn on in different combinations at different times. Rather than ending up with a set of 'illustrations' that map one-to-one onto Bible stories, the mental and spiritual resource bank will be more like *that drawer* in the kitchen (we all have one): everything that might possibly be useful goes in there, so that we can reach into it when we need to and find the right thing. And we don't have to use everything at once! It's OK to save some ideas for next time.

This means that if we need to go off-script in a talk to respond to something, the things that pop into our heads on the spur of the moment are not coming from nowhere, but from the rich bank of theological and spiritual wisdom that we've been accumulating.

> We may feel like we're making a talk up on the spot, but we've potentially been preparing it all our life.

It may take time to build up the confidence to change tack mid-sermon based on a contribution from the congregation, but as some of the reflections in this book will show, it can be amazingly rewarding when we do. Approached in this way, the process that begins with planning to preach continues in the delivery and, as we see below, into the way that we reflect on and learn from each experience.

3 Reviewing our practice

Preaching with all ages can be tiring – it asks a lot of us. Often the last thing we want to do afterwards is pick over what happened. But getting into the habit of reviewing our practice is what helps us learn. Preaching with all ages can be unpredictable, and what happened may not have been quite what we planned – reviewing and reflecting on an experience can help make sense of it and draw out good and fruitful learning even when it didn't go as we'd hoped.

It can be helpful to invite a couple of people we trust to offer feedback. Choose carefully – hopefully there will be some people in the congregation or ministry team who will offer honest, constructive comments, including encouragement, both from their own perspective and how they perceived others engaging with the talk.

Remember, it may take congregations (as well as preachers) a little time to get used to a more interactive style. If we don't get lots of responses at first, we mustn't give up – it's well worth persevering.

The following prompts may help guide this process of reflecting and reviewing. There is a photocopiable version of this table at the end of the book.

What did I want to happen, and why?	What actually happened, and why?
What was better than I hoped?	What didn't go as well as I hoped?
What did I learn about myself?	What did I learn about my congregation/context?
What did I learn about God?	What do I want to add to my 'rummage' drawer?

4. Formation

Looking back at steps 1 to 3 when you have given and reflected on several talks, ask yourself what patterns are emerging, and what themes and ideas you find yourself returning to or pondering. What do you do differently now, and what deeper learning can you identify? How have you changed as a person and as a preacher? Sharing your ongoing learning with a friend or ministry colleague can help you to articulate some of this.

In summary …

Planning	Action	Reflection	Formation
Discerning the gospel in the gospel for our context to shape what we will offer in our all-age preaching slot.	Delivering the talk so as to enable others to join us in exploring scripture, theology and life experiences, encountering God together and growing in faith.	Reflecting on our practice, with 'mistakes' as part of the process, valuing and learning from the unexpected – about God, our congregation and ourselves.	Embedding habits and practices over time, identifying key themes and values that will shape our ministry, our faith and our context.

3

Reflecting on the storm and the cushion

In Mark 4.35–41 we read about Jesus sleeping on a cushion in the boat while his disciples are frantic at a raging storm, convinced they are going to die. They are fishermen – they know how quickly water can become dangerous. They also know scripture. They remember how God separated the land from the chaotic waters at creation: a storm feels like the chaos breaking through again. Does God no longer care, or is he powerless to act? Jesus' nap feels like a betrayal. Does *he* not care? When they wake him, of course he makes short work of the wind and the waves, and gently questions their lack of faith.

The first time I preached on this passage in an all-age context I homed in on the cushion on which Jesus slept, because it seemed an incongruous detail. In a highly sensory Gospel reading, the cushion stood out in contrast with the power of the elements and the visceral nature of the danger. I let the image of the cushion in the storm come into conversation with the sorts of metaphorical storms that congregation members might be facing, and perhaps my own insecurities as someone fairly new to preaching. The gospel in the gospel that I identified was to help the congregation discern ways, despite life's challenges, to find our rest in God.

As I worked out how to do this, the cushion proved helpful. I remembered that Joan, an elderly woman in the congregation, had said to me that if I ever needed anything sewing, I could ask her. I approached her to see if she would be willing to make a large number of tiny soft cushions – enough for one each on the Sunday. They were even better than I'd hoped: small, plump, squashy and unique, as she'd used odd bits of leftover fabric from her scrap bag.

Having arranged a boat shape out of chairs, and placed a large floor cushion in the middle, we acted out the storm using sound effects as the Gospel was read, and then focused on the cushion and wondered together what it meant for Jesus to be able to rest and relax while the storm raged, and what it might mean for us. As I passed the basket of cushions round, inviting people to take one and hold it, we thought together about what some of the storms might be in our own lives and what helps us to get through them. Who comforts us, and how? We spoke of prayer, of knowing that we are loved, of turning the pillow over after a nightmare to stop it coming back, of hope, and of the love of God. We looked at Jesus sleeping, and saw what it means to be at ease in God's love in a way that we don't often manage ourselves. Some people shared their own experiences of feeling that God was far away, and what helped them to realize that God was in the boat with them. It was a conversation in which we learned from one another's lived experience of what it means to trust in God in good times and in bad.

This was one of those times when standing to say the creed felt like a natural response to the story and our reflections on it: 'Where is your faith?' asked Jesus, and we could respond, 'We believe …'. Everyone held their cushions in the creed, and kept hold of them during the prayers. They were a tangible reminder of the trust in God that Jesus modelled, asleep in the boat.

We left the handful of spare cushions in a basket by the door: as with the leftover food at the feeding of the five thousand there was blessing enough to spare for those who were not in the crowd that day, so at the end of the service I said that if anyone knew someone who could do with hearing the story we had shared that morning, they were welcome to take a cushion and pass it on, along with the story.

oOoOo

On another occasion we used this scripture and the image of the cushion as the focus for a service for younger children and their parents/carers. Each person was given a plain pillow case, and they used fabric pens to decorate it in some way that would remind them of the love of God for them. There were some sample prayers adapted from the ancient service of Compline (Night Prayer)[1] that the children could ask their adult to write on the pillow case, or they could draw symbols such as hearts, crosses, smileys, rainbows, and so on – or just scribble decorations on it, while we talked together about what makes us feel safe. They were encouraged to take their pillow case home and use it on the pillow on their own bed – inside whatever pillow case they usually used. Nobody else would know it was there, but they would know, and perhaps, like Jesus in the storm, it would help them to rest in the love of God.

Pastorally speaking, the cushion was a powerful image in both contexts because it did not in fact focus on the calming of the storm, but of the reality of God's presence *within* the storm. Jesus is in the boat too. He has not abandoned anyone. The storm still rages, and God still loves. The storm is not a sign that God is powerless or uncaring, for the wind and the waves are also part of creation, held in God's almighty hands. This is why the creed made sense between the preaching and the intercessions in church: we were able to hold together our faith in God and the reality that life was, for many people there, far from easy. We did not have to deny the storm in order to proclaim our faith or receive God's love. The creed helped us let God be God: God's almighty nature does not depend on us having a good day, or an easy life. But through the Incarnation, when Jesus lived on earth as God-with-us, we see that God is both almighty and vulnerable with us in the storms that often beset us in our human experience. God is in the boat with us

Reflecting back, I wondered about the experience of saying the

---

1 See, for example, the liturgy included in the Church of England's daily prayer feed: www.churchofengland.org/prayer-and-worship/join-us-daily-prayer.

creed for those whose faith was at a very early stage or who were going through a more prolonged wilderness period. I had worried, retrospectively, about whether connecting the creed so strongly with the talk had been manipulative, moving people too quickly into a statement of faith. What reassured me about this was the communal nature of the creed: not only is Jesus with us in the boat, but so are our fellow disciples who, like the original Twelve, are at very different stages of faith and understanding. Perhaps there are times when we ourselves find it's hard to say 'I believe', and the faith of our fellow travellers helps us through.

One approach to theological reflection emphasizes an embodied engagement with experience, paying particular attention to the senses and emotions.[2] Out of this embodied engagement with experience an image or symbol comes into focus, which is then put into conversation with theological tradition, with the experience itself and any wider issues, using whatever sources of wisdom are helpful. Out of that conversation insight is generated, leading to action and transformation.

The stilling of the storm is a highly embodied story, visceral and powerful, and full of contrasts. As I entered into this story, the image that arose for me was that of the cushion. Like most symbols, the cushion had a range of possible resonances and meanings. I felt, with the Disciples, a sense of betrayal – how can Jesus rest while we are in danger? At the same time the cushion drew me because that peace that Jesus had I wanted for myself. At the time I first preached this text, I was a new mum, and I was familiar both with the desperate desire for sleep and with a real jealousy of anyone around me who seemed to be getting the rest I needed! So there was something personal in this for me that drew me to the cushion image, though I'm not sure I was aware of it at the time.

But I also recognized in it something more universal. The notion of peace amid chaos resonated through scripture – from Elijah

---

2 See especially the approach described in Patricia O'Connell Killen and John de Beer, *The Art of Theological Reflection*, New York: Crossroad, 1994.

finding unexpected rest in the wilderness and then meeting God in the silence, hidden in the cleft of the rock,[3] to the institution of the Sabbath,[4] to the psalms,[5] to Jesus' usually futile attempts to find some peace and quiet to pray, away from the crowds.[6]

Outside of scripture, and perhaps also reflecting my life experience at the time, I was reminded of comfort blankets and soft toys, and the feeling of a well-worn comfy jumper, an old quilt – perhaps it helped, here, that the cushions were made from quilting scraps (as so often is the case, the chance details of the medium end up providing extra layers of meaning). I was as confident as I could be that the image of the cushion would connect with a wide range of people at a symbolic level, as well as clearly on a literal level.

The cushions worked so well because they were highly sensory – they were not so much encouraging an intellectual response as a physical, emotional, spiritual response. As we reflected together as a congregation we were able to connect our emotional and intellectual and spiritual responses through a symbol that was sensory, rich and resonant, and the whole process became genuinely transformative.

This was also one of the first all-age talks I'd ever done, and certainly the first that really worked. I wonder, looking back, how much that Gospel story was an opportunity for me to learn to trust God to be with me so that I could remain calm amid the chaos of an all-age service. I now recognize that this experience was transformative for me as a preacher.

You can follow up some of these themes in:

Chapter 4: Engaging through the senses
Chapter 12: Medium and message, process and product
Chapter 20: Engaging with human experience

---

3 1 Kings 19.
4 Genesis 1.
5 Psalms 23, 91 and 121 have been especially helpful to me pastorally and in my own journey.
6 Mark 1.35–36.

4

Engaging through the senses

Rightly or wrongly, we might expect a sermon for adults to consist of one-sided talking, and that the congregation would be able to concentrate even if the sermon isn't terribly engaging. What might we do differently if we are hoping to engage a congregation that includes all ages? The most obvious thing is to use more than just words.

Human beings are embodied people – we are not just minds, or even souls. We are whole people and we live out our life and faith in a material world for which we bear responsibility and with which we interact every moment of every day. As Christians we believe in a God who 'became flesh and lived among us',[1] and the sacramental life of the Church reflects this holistic, embodied way of encountering God: we 'become what we receive'[2] at the Eucharist – the body of Christ. This is not to say that the Church has always had a healthy or balanced attitude to the body.[3] But if preaching with all ages gives us a licence to preach in a way that engages with the senses, we may be able to heal some of these lingering anxieties around being embodied, and this can be transformative for individuals and for communities.

---

1 John 1.14.

2 St Augustine, Easter Sermon 227.

3 David Brown's *God and Grace of Body* (Oxford: Oxford University Press, 2007) is a fascinating exploration of embodiedness in Christian tradition.

> 'You said that the bread and wine was an outward and visible sign of an inward and spiritual grace. But you were wrong. It's not because of what they look like. It's what they feel like. When you have the wine it feels warm all the way down, like a hug, like love. The warmth of the wine is a sign of God's love.' (age 7)

This child's insight into the sensory world of the sacraments is a helpful starting point. Adults who regularly drink alcohol may have forgotten how different a tiny sip of fortified wine feels from a sip of juice or milk.[4] On the other hand, adults who are used to wafers at Communion may forget to connect this with the comforting warmth of a freshly baked loaf of bread, and how this, too, may be a vehicle for God's love and blessing.[5] Engaging with our senses makes room for these kinds of experiences of God to be heard and valued in a way that might never happen if we did not reflect together.

If the talk or sermon is part of (not a break from) worship, then it is not just teaching *about* God but is an encounter *with* God; and if we find that we can enable people in our preaching to encounter God through the world of the senses and the language of symbols, then there is also a sacramental quality to preaching.

Sight

Pictures probably feel like the easiest sensory resource to draw on, and many preachers already use them, at least as visual aids.

---

4 And this might make us think about the possibility of *warm* grape juice, rather than cold, if we offer it to those who are not able to receive alcohol for any reason.

5 There is a church in Liverpool that has bread-making as the main activity of its worship and fellowship; see www.somewhere-else.org.uk.

- A visual image can focus attention – it's something to look at for those who find it easier to engage with a picture than with words, or as a 'hook' on which to hang the words.
- An illustrative picture offers an alternative way of communicating a moment in a biblical story – we can picture what it looks like.
- A picture might also help connect a Bible story with a familiar contemporary situation.
- Always make sure that you are intentional about when you display images – don't leave a picture in the background unless you want it there, or it may distract people from what you want them to focus on.

Already you may have made the scripture more inviting and accessible. But an image can do much more than this. Works of art can be incredibly powerful in drawing out people's imagination and 'inner theologian'.

- If a picture has an emotional impact it may engage people more deeply and more quickly than words alone – an evocative image invites us into the story.
- Really paying attention to things (whether artworks or natural objects, and whether or not we consider them to be beautiful) reminds us to look with love on the world – we learn to see beauty not only in those things that the world thinks are beautiful, but in *all* things.

When exploring the Summary of the Law, we made 'scopes' (one folded piece of paper, curled into a heart shape, and another piece of paper wrapped round it to hold it in place) and looked through them to try to learn what it might be like to look with love on everything that is made. We looked out of the windows at the sparrows in the trees, and down under the pews at the spiders and the dust; we looked at one another, and finally we looked in a mirror and saw ourselves.

They say that a picture is worth a thousand words, so when we use images in preaching we should expect them to add a lot to what is said. When you use a visual image, consider what it adds to your words – what can the picture do that your words alone cannot?

- Images with any artistic depth to them will leave plenty of room for wondering and reflection – even simple images can trigger the imagination.
- The very questions that the artist faced when they began their work can encourage a congregation to wonder about the same things: why this particular moment in the story, this viewpoint? Why that background, those colours? Why this story at all?

When we look at art, there is an almost infinite number of 'right' observations; there are very few, if any, 'wrong' suggestions. This means that engaging with artwork is a way of *doing* theology. The artist has started a process of wondering and interpreting, and invites the congregation to join in.

- Using several contrasting artistic interpretations of the same Bible story helps the congregation see that each artist has *interpreted* the story, rather than merely illustrated it – they have chosen how to portray that story.
- Different interpretations can coexist in the same story: a Bible passage can have more than one meaning. Learning this can be liberating for adults whose faith has been formed by narrow or simplified certainties – experiencing ambiguity and even doubt may be an essential stage in their ultimate growth in faith.
- Children may see different things from adults, paying attention to different details. Those who are new to faith may notice things that those very familiar with the Bible have forgotten are striking.

- Congregations may also make connections that the artist did not intend – this is also a gift. We may not be able to follow up every idea every time, but sometimes someone will unlock a truth that we, as preachers, might never have found on our own.

Writing about a church in Gateshead, Stephen Burns relates how artwork was used successfully to promote intergenerational conversation and encouragement:

> 'Sermons were often accompanied by projected artwork and were always followed by a brief time of communal reflection, "chaired" by either presider or assistant, though highly informal in tone. Children participated in these discussions alongside adults, and this reflective time was a chief means of shared catechesis in the congregation, often involving testimony and encouragement by one to others.'
>
> *Stephen Burns*[6]

A friend[7] overheard someone giving a gallery tour to some children, and noted the brilliant ways that he encouraged them to share their thoughts:

> 'He was encouraging them that their ideas and impressions are valid – "That's a good thought – what do you see that makes you think that?" And when the kid was reluctant because it might be "wrong", he just repeats, "Just tell me what you see that made you think that."
>
> He's accepted multiple answers to the same question, "Why do you think the artist chose to use so many colours?" Then he's connected it to their own artwork, saying that whenever they make art, they have choices about how they tell the story too.'
>
> *Margaret Pritchard Houston*

6 Stephen Burns, *Worship in Context: Liturgical Theology, Children and the City*, London: Epworth Press, 2006, p. 224.

7 I'm very grateful to Margaret Pritchard Houston for these and many other helpful insights and stories.

Art can function like a wonderfully open question. The more we look, the more we see. We need not be afraid of using contemporary, abstract art in an all-age context – and we don't need to limit ourselves just to art that is obviously scriptural.[8]

Images begin to resonate not only with what they portray, but with our own experience too. They may remind us of our own story and help us to connect ourselves with God's story.

We were using pictures to think together about the Eucharist.

Seeing a line drawing of the Israelites gathering the manna in the wilderness, one elderly member of the congregation exclaimed, 'Oh, it's just like what I remember!' It turned out she was actually present during the liberation of Holland at the end of the Second World War when she was a child: the planes overhead, which had previously meant danger, now brought salvation in the form of food supplies, dropped from the very same air. They called it 'manna from heaven' and it saved her life.

This personal story, triggered by the art, was shared by someone elderly, connecting life experience with theological tradition, liturgy and scripture, in a way that allowed all ages to grasp something of what it meant.

Practical considerations about *how* to share visual images with a congregation may also have an impact on how the image is received and how people are able to engage with it.[9]

- Projecting an image onto a big screen allows the image to be a focal point or (especially if it's projected throughout the service)

---

8 An excellent online resource for using art to engage with scripture is the *Visual Commentary on Scripture*, created by theologians, artists, biblical scholars and art historians, all working together: https://thevcs.org/.

9 Detailed information on copyright is outside the scope of this book, but there are many places now online where good quality images can be sourced and used freely, such as the National Gallery and Wikimedia, and anything offered under creative commons licences.

a background – make sure it's a high enough resolution image for the screen size.

- Printing copies of an image for members of the congregation to use individually can make it easier for more than one image to be viewed at once, or for a number of images to be shared between people, and for encouraging informal conversation – this may be easier for  those who don't feel confident sharing ideas in front of the whole congregation, and can also be a stage on the way to doing so.
- Printed images can also be engaged with quietly while the preacher is still talking; they may also be taken home at the end of the service.
- It can be powerful for someone who can see an image clearly to describe it for those with visual impairments – this needn't be just a practical matter, but can be built into the process of engaging with a piece of art, as everyone will notice different details and may have different emotional responses: try to encourage not just factual descriptions (eg, 'It's a painting of Simeon holding baby Jesus'[10]) but also offerings such as:

> 'It's really warm colours, but quite dark.'
> 'It's quite fuzzy and blurred, as if the artist hasn't got his glasses on.'
> 'It reminds me of when my grandad met my baby for the first time.'
> 'When I look at this it makes me feel loved, but kind of sad.'
> 'The older person looks as if they might be feeling overwhelmed.'
> 'There's another figure in the background, but I'm not sure who it is.'

---

10 The painting I have in mind is a late one by Rembrandt, which you can find here: www.wikiart.org/en/rembrandt/simeon-with-the-christ-child-in-the-temple.

To hear this done well, try listening to a BBC Radio 4 programme about visual art; a good speaker will present the art in a way that allows a clear and dynamic image to arise in the listener's mind. As with all things, this works best if we listen to a variety of different people describing what they see.

All this is possible without the congregation even picking up a pencil or a paintbrush – see Chapter 12 for an exploration of what can happen when we allow ourselves not just to *think* like an artist, but to *create* artful theology as a congregation.

Sound

Speaking

Sound is normal in church – in a standard service we may hear lots of spoken words, both individually by various ministers, readers, intercessors, etc., and also communally, if parts of the service are said by all. Preaching with all ages is an opportunity to hear a variety of voices – and especially those voices not usually heard.

In some churches there's a culture of children being 'seen but not heard' – or at least a desire for this on the part of some of the adults! The normal sounds made by children (wriggling, play, talking to their parent or carer) may be interpreted as noise, and greeted with an irritated 'shhh'. Changing a church culture so that everyone can enjoy worship together requires careful and sensitive handling and a lot of patience, but is essential to becoming a church that really does function as an intergenerational community.

- Make sure that the church has done everything possible to ensure that people who are hard of hearing can hear, even over background noise – and try to teach children not to shout into microphones that are connected to hearing loops, as this can be painful for hearing aid users.

- Can we redeem 'noise' into 'sound' by creating opportunities for children's voices to be heard in a positive way, such as asking questions, wondering aloud and offering ideas?
- Children's voices may be heard in front of the whole congregation or in conversational interactions – part of our role as preacher is to facilitate this.
- Once people have heard a child contribute helpfully to worship, prayer and theology, it's harder to hear that same voice as a nuisance – assumptions have changed and prejudices have been challenged.
- Children who are fully engaged tend to make fewer sounds that other people find distracting.

 Giving intentional value to voices that are often silenced (which of course goes beyond children's voices) is a powerful, prophetic act that impacts individuals and transforms the gathered people as the Body of Christ.[11]

Singing

Most services will include singing, with or without instrumental accompaniment, by individuals or groups or the whole congregation, and perhaps also instrumental music alone. As preachers we may or may not have any influence over the music, but either way it's worth thinking through how preaching and music relate to each other.[12] The talk may even be able to draw on turns of phrase from those songs

11 For a hugely insightful account of voice and gender, read Mary Beard's *Women and Power*, London: Profile Books, 2017.

12 The RSCM's *Sunday by Sunday* resource suggests hymns and songs that reflect the themes of the season as well as reflecting the specific readings in the lectionary. Many hymnals also include a scriptural and thematic index, and electronic hymn/song resources such as *Hymnquest* are searchable for scriptural reference and themes.

as a way of integrating it with the rest of the worship and capitalizing on the way music makes words more memorable and formational.

Research has shown that singing in groups releases oxytocin (the 'love hormone'), which may be a contributing factor to the power of song in worship.[13] What we sing tends to remain in the memory, and gains a sense of credibility, not just because of the music but because of the power of rhyme and rhythm. *The Lego Movie* was correct in suggesting that we perceive a thing to be 'true because it rhymes'.[14] Children are often taught rhymes to help remember things, such as days in each month – these methods work because we are all, to a certain extent, wired up to seek out patterns in order to process the sensory data that we receive.

So how does all this help with preaching?

- We can refer to songs that our congregation know already, connecting with something that's already part of their life of faith. For instance, the words to well-loved Christmas carols can help us preach during the missional family-friendly services around Christmas as they help us tap into something familiar for people who aren't otherwise fluent in churchy language.[15]
- We can unpack more of the potential in familiar words. How might you use 'Be near me, Lord Jesus' to help you preach about the mystery of the Incarnation? Or 'The hopes and fears of all the years are met in thee tonight' to connect the challenges of Jesus' own day with those we face in the contemporary world, and to lead into prayer?
- We might find that inviting people to reflect on a text that is very familiar to us (but not to them) helps us hear it afresh.

---

13 This is widely referenced, for example: www.frontiersin.org/articles/10.3389/fnhum.2015.00518/full.

14 *The Lego Movie*, Warner Animation Group, 2014.

15 Though it is worth really reading the text carefully to make sure you are clear about the theology being implied – carols are reflecting on the mystery of the Incarnation, and sometimes they sacrifice doctrinal accuracy for the sake of a memorable rhyme!

- We might try writing our own words to a tune that is well known and brings with it helpful associations; a tune associated with a particular season, or that has a particular 'mood', will affect how people experience any new words we may write.
- If we're really brave, we might try composing a song during the talk itself, perhaps using a formula, such as 'He's got the whole world in his hands' or 'Give me joy in my heart', getting the congregation to generate new verses as part of their reflection on scripture – see Chapter 12 for more on what can happen when we get creative with a different 'medium' from usual.
- If you have members of the Deaf community in your congregation, you may wish to have a conversation with them about signing in addition to singing – if a whole congregation can learn to sign a simple song, it can enable them to reflect more deeply on the meaning behind the words.[16] This is just one example of many ways in which we might use all-age preaching as a way of encouraging a more inclusive culture in church.

Other sounds

Instrumental music can also be effective in giving people space to think and reflect – without words, it may communicate powerfully in other ways, while leaving scope for individual response. Some churches have found that instrumental music can help people focus on a reflective activity – more so than silence.

---

16 'Away in a manger' is an interesting example, as the sign for the baby in verse 1 is different from the sign later in the song for the grown-up Jesus (which mimes the nail marks at the crucifixion); this can enable a congregation to connect the Christmas story with the big story of God's love for the world.

> One Holy Week the children and young people planned a reflection in place of the talk. We asked the congregation to close their eyes while we read a simplified version of the Passion story. There were no visual aids, just sounds, amplified through the microphone. For instance, when Jesus turned over the tables in the Temple we dropped big packing boxes on the floor, emptied a jar of coins, and ruffled the pages of a hymn book as the sound of the doves' wings. Having the sounds and the words, but nothing to see, made people attend to the story imaginatively.

Listening

Listening begins with paying attention – we can model this in the way that we pay attention to contributions that people make in our preaching. As a preacher it can be tempting to answer every question and respond to every idea straight away – but our pause for thought can be a gift to others as well as to ourselves. To hear others, we must first stop speaking, giving up the sound of our own voice.

When John Cage composed his famous '4:33' (a piece of music that requires the musicians to remain silent) he was challenging the audience to pay quality attention to all the sounds that are around us and that we usually ignore. I wonder what might happen if we used silence or times of quiet in an all-age talk. What sounds might we hear, and what meaning would those sounds have if we are treating them as something precious and worth paying attention to?

Silence buys us time: time to think and reflect, to process questions and ideas before sharing them. It gives space for those who process better internally, or who process things more slowly.

Silence isn't often associated with all-age worship, but it can happen – and 'quietness' can certainly happen. Try some of these approaches to hosting a time of quiet:

- Encourage people to listen to their own breathing (without breathing any more loudly!), or their own heartbeat; 'Become aware of yourself being in the presence of God.'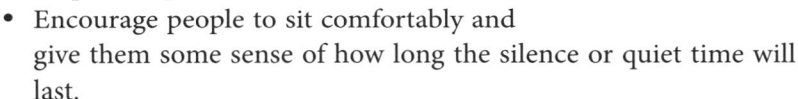
- Give people a thought to ponder, or something to imagine – this gives purpose and shape to a quiet time.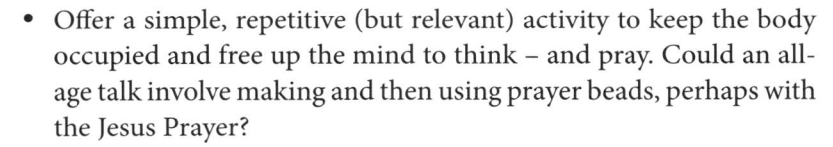
- Encourage people to sit comfortably and give them some sense of how long the silence or quiet time will last.
- Offer a simple, repetitive (but relevant) activity to keep the body occupied and free up the mind to think – and pray. Could an all-age talk involve making and then using prayer beads, perhaps with the Jesus Prayer?

Taste

Bread and wine

As we share the bread and wine we participate not only in Christ's death and resurrection, foreshadowed at the Last Supper, but also in all the planned and impromptu meals that Jesus shared with his friends, with his enemies, and with whatever random crowd of people were willing to sit and eat with him. From the feeding of the five thousand, to the barbequed fish on the beach after the resurrection, Jesus revealed who he was and who we are in the sharing of food. Eucharistic worship therefore draws not only on a specific meal that we have ritualized, but on a pattern of hospitality that may helpfully pervade our whole life as Christian communities.

Saying grace before meals, collecting donations for food banks, hosting coffee mornings, arranging harvest collections of food for homeless shelters, and so on, are all part of this. Even the coffee and squash and biscuits after a service in some way participate in this

'bigger eucharistic celebration' that escapes from the liturgy and flavours our lives. Embracing this is just as important for churches in which children may receive communion as for those where they aren't able to do so.[17] What we can do is pay attention to the sacramental life of the church in its broadest possible sense, and affirm the part that eating and drinking – as a community – might play in the journey of discipleship for people of all ages.

Eating in preaching

'Taste and see that the Lord is good.' (Psalm 34)

Sharing food in an all-age sermon takes some planning and care, especially when we take into account food hygiene concerns, intolerances and allergies, as well as lifestyle and dietary preferences, so it's best not to be over-ambitious the first time you try it!

- Gluten, animal products (including dairy) and nuts are the major culprits here.
- Watch out for lesser known allergies, such as mustard seeds (unfortunately!).
- Grapes should be halved lengthways to avoid a potential choking hazard.
- Some people genuinely can't eat certain 'healthy' fresh foods.

17 Practice varies between denominations and even between different churches of the same denomination. A good starting point for thinking these decisions (and their implications) through is this article by Margaret Pritchard Houston: www.london.anglican.org/articles/the-body-of-christ-given-for-you/.

- Allergies can be life-threatening, so if in doubt err on the side of caution, always warn people just before you start (or at the start of the service if you can), and make it clear that nobody absolutely *has* to taste or eat what you're offering.

Daily raisins

Raisins are usually a fairly safe bet for all but the smallest children (though do check, and have alternatives available – my nephew is allergic to them …), and can be a useful and inexpensive means of taking time to taste the goodness of God.

> One Lent, my church used the story of the manna from heaven and the 'daily bread' line in the Lord's Prayer to reflect on the daily blessings of God. We gave out a small packet of raisins to each person, with a label on the box: 'one a day: eat as you pray'. In the talk we each took a raisin from our box, and ate it slowly, letting it almost dissolve, enjoying its sweetness, while we thought about the blessings we have received from God, and the blessings we longed for. The rest of the pack was to take home – there were about 35 to 40 raisins per pack, so one pack would last a month until the next all-age service. The intention was to use the sense of taste to slow down and make intentional time – even if only a minute – to come before God in prayer and in thanksgiving, and in a way that enabled the talk to have lasting impact beyond the service.

Chocolate

I have yet to do this in a sermon, but one day I hope to lead a chocolate-tasting session to accomplish something similar and rather more decadent.

> Enjoy the packaging, read the ingredients, feel the quality of the foil, dwell on the sheen of the chocolate's surface …
>
> Smell it as you might with a nice wine, snap it to listen to its texture …
>
> Finally put it in your mouth – if you hold your nose until the chocolate has started to melt, then let go, you'll get the full aroma and taste at the same time!

How might you use this to help people practise attentiveness?

How might you use a chocolate tasting in a Fairtrade Fortnight or harvest service to encourage a sense of value and thanksgiving for the food we eat? Could you source chocolate that uses sustainable palm oil? And something that would be safe for people with diabetes and those who are dairy free?

Making and sharing

Preaching with the sense of taste can also be a powerful experience, especially when it involves gestures of giving and receiving and sharing – what we 'practise' in church, we can then do in the rest of life.

It is well worth looking at resources from Traidcraft (for Fairtrade Fortnight), WaterAid, Christian Aid and other development agencies for reflective ideas using food, which often focus not only on sharing resources but on cherishing and valuing them.

Whatever you do with food in church, make sure that it sends out a message that food is precious, and not something to be wasted: if you make a smoothie or toast or biscuits in a talk, make them in such a way that they can be eaten and shared, and try to make sure you have an alternative for those with allergies. Anything that needs washing (such as grapes) should be washed before the service, and for smaller children grapes need halving lengthways so that they are not a choking hazard.

Scent

Churches have their own smells, depending on the style and age of the building and how it's used: polish, incense, damp, dust, coffee … Of all the senses, this may be the most challenging to incorporate into preaching, but it is often said to be the sense that triggers memories and emotional responses most readily. Scent is also closely related to taste (as above in the description of chocolate tasting) so you may well find that if you use food in worship you are also engaging with people's sense of smell.

During a flower festival, we used Matthew 6.25–33 to reflect on the transient, fragile nature of creation and our responsibility for its care. In the talk we went for a walk around the church, taking in all the beautiful displays with our senses. In particular, the scent of roses and freesias was something that couldn't be created artificially, and was a sign for us, as we looked at and smelt all the beautiful arrangements, of God's creativity and abundant grace.

'I did a whole all-age sermon based on different smells. The church was going through Lent using the senses, and my week was the story of Nicodemus visiting Jesus in the night using smell! Each family was given a bag of smells as they arrived: e.g. 'sage' because Nicodemus was supposed to be wise, 'baby shampoo' on a piece of cotton wool, as we talked about being born again, and some spices, as we later talked about how Nicodemus obviously thought about all he'd learned and later was one of those to bury Jesus. We then used 'scratch and sniff' stickers during the prayers. Although at the time if felt like we might have been pushing some of the connections, it ended up going really well and was very memorable. The congregation also got to take their bags of smells home with them, which enabled them to remember the story better.'

Chris Campbell

Touch

One way to use their sense of touch in preaching is to invite people to undertake a simple activity during a period of listening or silence, or while they have a conversation. For some people, having something sensory to do while they talk and listen helps them to focus their attention. For instance:

- One Good Friday I handed out small roughly cut wooden crosses and small squares of sandpaper, so that during a time of reflection following the Gospel reading (the story of the crucifixion), people could sand down the rough edges of their cross. This helped people focus their minds on the cross as a symbol, and opened up some interesting questions:

  Do we 'sanitize' the cross symbolically, forgetting the brutal reality of Jesus' own cross?

  Can the splinters and sharp edges help us to recall Jesus' suffering? As we sand down the rough edges with care and diligence, are we echoing in some way the women's desire to tend gently to Jesus' body?

- In one of my churches we had a 'blanket of blessing' – a soft, dark red fleecy blanket, which our toddler service used sometimes for the prayers. We used it once in an all-age service, confident that the toddlers and their parents and carers would recognize it and help the rest of the congregation use it. The talk was about the way that God blesses us through one another, and the activity was simply that one person would take the blanket and wrap it round someone else (who had indicated they would like it!) and say, 'God bless you.' The person who had been blessed would then take the blanket and pass it on to someone else in the same way. In a cold church, this worked both symbolically and literally as a form of blessing. With the blanket's softness and warmth, and the human contact, full of goodwill, form and content combined effectively – so much so that one older person was reluctant to pass the blanket on! Many churches have a prayer shawl ministry, or make blankets for the homeless or those in hostels, with the sense that it is the whole congregation, not just the maker of the blankets, who are praying and blessing.

Touch is also hugely important for people with visual impairments or other disabilities that may make it hard for them to access other forms of interaction. I have seen visual art become tactile in the hands of someone who cannot see it, and wonderful insights emerge from touching and holding an object, rather than just looking at it. I have also learned from someone with profound disabilities whose carer has helped them, through touch, to engage with an activity and so enabled them both – and the congregation – to encounter God.

Using the senses in worship and in preaching – maybe not all in the same service, but at least over time – opens up theology in new ways, and may also offer opportunities to include those who may not often be included. If a 'visual aid' is not just visual but is also multisensory, it enables those with visual impairments not only to be included but to offer their particular perspective and witness without which the whole Body of Christ is impoverished.

Too much?

> We went to a new church for the first time, and some-one said to me, 'See that door – that's the room we set aside for anyone who feels overwhelmed and needs some calm time – you're welcome to use it if you need to.' It was really thoughtful – it turned out that the church congregation included several children on the autistic spectrum, for whom the 'retreat room' was essential for their well-being and full inclusion in church.

'Neurodiversity' is used to encompass the range of ways that people may interact and process sensory and other data, including people who would identify as autistic. Some children and adults find particular kinds of (or larger amounts of) sensory stimulation or interaction overwhelming. As a preacher, you can help in a few ways:

> In my previous church we converted the room under the tower to a comfy quiet room. It had a large window into the church so you could still see what was happening, and if you switched the speakers on you could hear, too.

- Explain what you're planning to do so that anyone who might find it difficult is prepared – but make sure you don't overwhelm people with too many instructions.
- Have a space where anyone overwhelmed can retreat to if they need it.
- Get to know your congregation – what is helpful for one person may not be so for another. Ask them to help you plan what you're going to do.

> **All may, some should, none must.** Allow people the option of participating in a less active way, or in a way that doesn't demand that they leave their comfort zone if they're not in a place emotionally to do so that day.

Try the exercises on the opposite page.

Hold a piece of string or ribbon.
Describe it in every way you can
– its physical properties and its uses.
What memories and meanings does it offer you?
What attributes have potential for exploring the gospel?

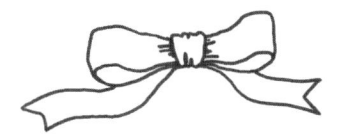

Pick up a stone, and pay attention to it.
Describe it, noting what it has in common
with all stones, and what is unique.
What happens as you hold it?
What attributes of stones – or this stone –
resonate with stories or images from scripture?

Try to find a small log
or part of the branch of a tree,
and hold it in your hands.
Feel all the different textures.
Does it have a distinctive smell?
What about its colours and patterns?
What is the grain of the wood like?
What kind of tree is it from?
What will it be used for?
How do trees and wood feature
in scripture and theology?

5

Reflecting on relationships

I prepared some not-too-sharp scissors and three long, beautiful ribbons which had been left behind after a wedding that had taken place in church.

I retold the story of the prodigal son, asking three people who happened to be sitting roughly in a triangle to hold the end of a ribbon in each hand, so that the ribbons also formed a triangle. I explained that the story was about a family – a father, an older son and a younger son – and played up how beautiful and special the ribbons were, representing their relationships.

When we got to the moment when the younger son broke away from the family, I cut the ribbon between him and the father, so that the frayed ends of the ribbon hung down, limp  and broken. We paused to feel sad or angry or shocked at destroying something so beautiful.

We reached the point when the younger son returned, seeking not to be part of the family but a servant. We held the two frayed ends near each other, in hope. But effectively, the father says: 'If you come home then you come as my son – there is no place for you here as my servant, only as my child.' The younger son had to decide what to do. He chose to mend the broken pieces and become a son again. I then tied up the frayed ends of the ribbon in a bow. The two people holding them found they had to lean closer to each other as the bow meant there was less length of ribbon between them.

Then we reached the point where the older son rejects his brother and his father, at which point I cut the other two ribbons. We paused, again, lamenting what had been destroyed.

Jesus left the story unfinished, so that we have to finish it ourselves. The congregation were desperate for me to tie the frayed ends together, as we had with the first one, but we stopped before we did that and wondered what it would take in real life for this to happen. Not just apologies, but forgiveness, love, humility … And sometimes we have to work hard to become ready. We have to be willing to lean, or even move, towards one another.

When we finally did tie all the loose ends together, we noticed how the three people were standing much closer than before, and how the ribbons, tied in bows, were even more beautiful than they had been at first.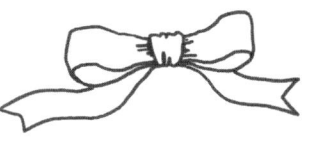

∘◯∘◯∘

I have used this story and the ribbons on a number of occasions. It has always been powerful, and as such it comes with a health warning: enacting a story like this is akin to psychodrama (drama therapy), which is a powerful tool for analysing and reflecting on complex (especially relational) experiences. Psychodrama requires experienced facilitation, and it may leave people feeling vulnerable. When a similar 'enacted' process is used of a biblical narrative, we may think it's 'safe' because it's about a fictional family from two thousand years ago; this is not the case. Rather, the relational patterns being played out in the parable are familiar, to a greater or lesser extent, to many families, and the enactment of the drama, including the pain of the ribbons being cut, the sense of isolation, the yearning for reconciliation, the resentment and bitterness and the difficulty of stepping towards one another may resonate powerfully with people whose own family relationships have something in common with the prodigal's family.

I have learned the hard way that this story, especially when acted out, requires very sensitive handling. Whenever we engage in activities that may resonate powerfully with people's experiences, we must be sensitive to their potential vulnerability, careful and gentle in the way that we explore, and prepared to follow up pastorally as necessary.

I have also found that some people need to stay longer with the frayed ends of their ribbons, acknowledging the complexity and unresolved nature of many relationships. During prayer the frayed ends can be used as a sensory symbol enabling us to hold before God those things that are in need of reconciliation and healing.

Many people would argue that we should avoid addressing difficult areas in our preaching with all ages, but my experience has been that as long as we are careful and accountable it can be entirely appropriate to do so: if we only ever skate over the surface of human experience, we risk suggesting that there are whole aspects of our lives that we cannot bring before God, and we risk selling the gospel short.

Opening up such areas during preaching at least means that we are able to follow up with prayer, and with the support of a loving community. But we also need to be aware that for many people church is not (yet) a place where they feel free to explore or express strong emotion. Preaching with all ages using sensory, embodied means can touch people deeply.

I have used the same activity, but without the story, to explore relationship with God and with one another generally in the liturgical context of confession and absolution. Without the story to personalize it, this is still a powerful activity, but carries less emotional risk.

Whenever we preach, we need to be aware that what we are doing may connect with people in ways that make them vulnerable. Preaching always carries with it the responsibility to offer appropriate pastoral care.

You can follow up some of these themes in:

Chapter 4: Engaging through the senses
Chapter 6: Engaging in different ways
Chapter 13: Reflecting on scripture
Chapter 16: Engaging with liturgy and worship
Chapter 20: Engaging with human experience.

6

Engaging in different ways

You may well be familiar with the idea of learning styles – that different people process and engage in different ways. The learning we do during an all-age talk may include learning about God, but hopefully it is also about coming to know God more deeply and understanding who we are as God's people. Learning, in this deeper sense, is a significant part of the process, and the New Testament Greek word translated 'disciple' simply means 'learner'.

A simple version of the learning styles theory suggests that people can learn visually (looking – such as reading a book), aurally (hearing – such as going to a lecture) and kinaesthetically (doing – trying it out). More complex versions might include:

- **Interpersonal** – processing ideas through interaction with others, conversation and questions.
- **Intrapersonal** – processing through personal reflection, during an uninterrupted time of quiet.
- **Visual** – using images and pictures, from high art to diagrams and doodles.
- **Verbal** – making sense of ideas through words, either written or spoken.
- **Musical/rhythmic** – learning and making sense of ideas through rhythmic and musical patterns.
- **Kinaesthetic** – processing and learning by 'doing'.

- **Logical/mathematical** – seeking order in new ideas through cause and effect and logic.

The idea of learning styles is now treated with some suspicion: neurologically, the different parts of our brains are so interconnected that our learning is not as compartmentalized as learning style theory would suggest. It's also been shown that teaching according to preferred learning style doesn't improve learning outcomes. If we are encouraged to 'pigeonhole' ourselves by learning style, we may start to believe that there is *only one* way that we can learn. In truth, most of us can learn and engage in a whole variety of ways, and different ways of presenting and processing ideas can generate different insights, to everyone's benefit.

Spiritual styles

A more helpful model may be the idea of spiritual styles, developed by David Csinos.[1] According to his research, there are four main styles that capture how children and adults encounter God:  word-centred, emotion-centred, symbol-centred and action-centred, and each of us will be more comfortable with some than others.

A word-centred approach values clarity and precision: 'they know God when they know about God'. This approach will likely centre on cognitive learning, including exegetical preaching and Bible study,

1 You can read more about this framework and access some excellent resources (from which the following summaries have been adapted) via the links on this page: www.going4growth.com/growth_in_faith_and_worship/ spirituality/spiritual-styles. See also www.rootsontheweb.com.

personal study and instructional teaching, with the Bible as central to Christian faith.

An emotion-centred approach 'upholds feelings as the core of spirituality' and values the process of exploring experiences deeply. This approach may draw on the performing arts as a way of expressing feelings, and focus on personal relationship with Jesus.

A symbol-centred approach is essentially mystical, using symbols, images and metaphors to worship God who is, ultimately, 'beyond our understanding'. This approach focuses on wonder and awe, particularly in response to the natural world and to art, or in times of silence or meditation.

An action-centred approach focuses on what 'brings about positive transformation in the world', in which spirituality is primarily lived out in the world and God is encountered in the needs of the world.

I know I recognize aspects of my own spirituality in the above descriptions. We all have a slightly different combination of preferences and a slightly different-shaped comfort zone when it comes to encountering God, whether in preaching or in other circumstances. What works for one person won't work so well for another. Can you possibly meet everyone's needs at once?

- Although most of us gravitate towards some ways of engaging more than others, most of us can manage a whole variety. Aim for a varied diet over time – don't always do the same thing, but don't be afraid of some repetition, too.
- The idea isn't to pigeonhole people into a 'type' and to provide something narrowly specific for them, but to offer people a balance between what's in their comfort zone and what will challenge them – this is one of the ways that we grow spiritually. Can we offer some choice, and then bring together what different groups have worked on in different ways?

- As preachers we do need to ensure that we're not just gravitating to our own preferred style – otherwise we risk communicating that our way of encountering God is *the* way, and those who can't easily engage with God that way may feel disenfranchised and discouraged. We can learn a huge amount from how others engage – and expand our own comfort zone.
- Realizing that other people encounter God in different ways is a key piece of learning for children (and indeed adults), and being willing to join in with something because it's good for someone else, even if it's not our style, is a sign of maturity in the Body of Christ.
- We can look out for those who we know might find something we have planned challenging.
- We can experiment with ways of engaging that can appeal to a variety of people, for example teaching and learning a new skill, such as plaiting.
- We can seek out ways of engaging in which the process and the 'content' are both giving out the same message – for example, collaborative activities that depend on diverse people working together lend themselves to teaching about the Kingdom and the nature of Christian community (see Chapter 12 for more on this).

It's not just preaching that needs to take into account the variety of ways that people engage – worship, discipleship and church life generally can also benefit from such an understanding. Our preaching with all ages can help model good practice as we affirm the variety of ways of engaging as a sign of the diversity of the Body of Christ.

In Genesis 1.27, 'In the image of God he created them, male and female he created them', we are presented with an understanding of anthropology in which people are made in the image of God not *despite* their differences but *collectively because of their differences*. It is by virtue of our diversity that we are, *together*, God's image. In preaching with all ages – and all styles – we are not only seeking to engage *each* person so that they can encounter God more deeply, but we are also seeking to engage a whole congregation of people

together in a communal act of
encounter between God and
the Body of Christ. Honour-
ing the diversity of people in
a congregation is a scriptural
imperative, and a theological
principle in itself.[2]

All bodies and minds are different. We each need to work out in
our own context, sensitively and almost certainly through conversation and listening, what will feel affirming and empowering.[3]

- Not everyone's body works well, or as they would like it – some
  disabilities are visible and some can't be seen.
- People's minds work differently too – neurodiversity, as a term,
  acknowledges diversity without necessarily implying disability.[4]
- Dementia may make it hard for someone to follow what's happening, whether the sermon is all-age or not.[5]
- Not all people with disabilities feel the same way about their disability and how it relates to their identity.
- Not everyone feels positively about their body even if it seems like
  a perfectly good body to the people around them.
- A human body and mind do not have to conform to a particular
  'norm' in order to be beautiful and beloved of God.

---

2 See also 1 Corinthians 12.

3 It's also well worth following up the resources here: http://disabilityandjesus.
org.uk/ and www.inclusive-church.org/disability.

4 Many churches have produced excellent guidelines on becoming more
autism-friendly, such as http://churchesforall.org.uk/about-disabled-people-
and-church/autism-spectrum/.

5 There is starting to be some excellent research and resourcing on dementia-
friendly churches, including this, from the Methodist Care Homes: www.mha.
org.uk/files/3814/0931/8295/Growing_Dementia_Friendly_Churches.pdf.

When we preach with all ages we can look for opportunities to affirm all the different ways in which we are human, as well as what we have in common, as people beloved of God and with a part to play in the Body of Christ.

> 'I have found that the key is to be as open-ended as possible, to leave as much space as possible for people to engage at whatever level they are at (which is not necessarily a reflection of chronological age).'
>
> *Ruth Harley*

> 'For me, the key thing in all-age worship is how people of different ages can participate in ways that are appropriate for their ages. Talks/activities need to be multi-layered so that a young child may be learning that church is a community of acceptance and fun, an older child may learn that they can make a contribution, and an adult may learn something else entirely.'
>
> *Robert Barlow*

7

Reflecting by the well

This was one of the messier things I've tried. I brought along some cups, a large jug of water, some sheets of shiny card from a Scrapstore,[1] and a large waterproof mat. Also, a plastic bucket with some small holes in the side towards the bottom (made by a heated skewer).

We recapped highlights from the story of the woman at the well, from John 4. These were largely the first part of the conversation, the bits about the living water and the mission to the city. We thought about how the people in the city may have thought of the woman as a bit of a leaky bucket – battered and broken, and not much good for anything – but how Jesus saw her potential.

We then used the apparatus to explore the living water. Several of us worked together to make a marble-run-style water feature, with the bucket at the top and the sheets of card bent round to make channels, lined up with the holes in the bucket, and the cups at the other end.

We poured the water, hearing and seeing it run down the channels and into the cups. We thought about times we use water in worship, such as at baptism. When we poured water into the bucket, it flowed out through the 'leaks' in slightly unpredictable ways but still ended up flowing down the channels and

---

1 A Scrapstore is a local community resource that recycles materials that have often been donated by local businesses – offcuts, surplus stock, and so on.

into the cups: there is often something haphazard and 'risky' about sharing the faith; it is opportunistic and can make us feel vulnerable.

We kept pouring for a bit. We tried some different configurations. We wondered about what would happen if the bucket was even leakier. We wondered what it would take for the water to reach the people at the very back of the church, reflecting on how the woman ran all the way back to her city and enabled them all to be refreshed with the living water.

Later I found myself drawn towards one particular aspect of this activity. The key players in this activity largely represented two groups in the church congregation. One group was very little children, and the other was retired men. The men were very active indeed in the church in practical ways: many of them were engaged in a long and complex project to build an extension to the church, which would give us running water, a kitchen and toilets, and a space to offer hospitality.[2] I mean, they were literally building it – with their bare hands. Many of them were retired engineers and were now using their skills to create something beautiful, functional and transformative for their church and community.

Thematically and symbolically, this talk connected with them at a number of levels. First, the 'water feature' activity drew on their knowledge of engineering – there were conversations about water flow, gravity, leaky pipes, and so on. It was an opportunity for them to bring their gifts not only into the church as a community, which they were already doing through the extension project, but into worship and preaching specifically. Second, the whole extension project was about enabling the church to be more hospitable. At the most basic level, it was about bringing running water into the ancient building in order that we might offer Christ's hospitality to local people and visitors from further afield, and be able to minister to all our visitors as if they were Christ himself.

The story of the woman at the well provided a rich conversation partner for this whole aspect of the church's life, enabling us to bring

---

2 You can read more about this project in Chapter 17: Reflecting on the stones.

into worship the very practical reality of stone and lime mortar, storm drains and window fittings that had been the focus of church life for many in the congregation. The woman's story connected with them particularly because what begins as a practical encounter based on hospitality becomes a rich spiritual and theological conversation, and ultimately an astonishing story of mission and transformation.

The next time I needed to engage with this Gospel reading in an all-age service, I was down to preach in the theological college where I was a tutor. The college community had a number of children, of varying ages and with varying degrees of theological knowledge. In preparation for the service we gathered the children a couple of weeks beforehand, and read the Gospel reading through together. It's a long reading, and we read it slowly, pausing every time we got to a bit that didn't make sense, or to a good stopping point, and talked about what we'd heard, asking questions and wondering aloud. Some of the children stayed for the whole conversation, while others wandered in and out.

As we undertook this process together we began to realize that we could do the same in the service – so we planned to have a very long and drawn-out Gospel procession, moving first to the font (which one of the children pointed out was the closest thing we had to a well), then to the nave, then to the altar.

At each point we planned to have a portion of the reading, followed by a 'micro-sermon' offered by one of the children. The micro-sermons were developed from the very questions that they had been asking as we met to plan the service:

'The Gospel says, if someone is thirsty, it doesn't matter who you are, and who they are, even if it's Jesus himself, you should just give them a drink.'	'In a way, Jesus is like the woman's husband, the husband that she should have had, because he accepts her as she is and actually loves her.'

The micro-sermons started to coalesce into a single theme: what does it mean to encounter and worship God? The well had drawn them to reflect on baptism, while the Disciples and the bread led them to reflect on the Eucharist – both intentional ways in which we encounter God. But the whole Gospel story is based on a chance encounter, where one person asked another for help. What the children had discerned is that encountering God can happen in unexpected places and people as well as in predictable, deliberate ways, and that it meant caring for others as well as being 'spiritual'.

We then opened the conversation to the whole congregation, ending up with the question, again from the children: is it possible for *everything* we do to be worship? We didn't try to answer this question, but left it for people to reflect on.

Thinking back to this event later, I was struck by the particular children involved and their perspective. Their parents were training for ministry, so they were used to a *lot* of church – and a lot of church services. They knew that worship was important, and though much of the worship in a theological college is not designed for children, many of them, for practical reasons, ended up coming to chapel. The question 'How should we be worshipping?' was a live one for them. I found it interesting that their micro-sermons focused not on the narrow definition of worship, but on the broader understanding of how worship connects with the rest of life: what does worship have to say about hospitality and need? How does our faith contribute to our relationships? How is faith expressed in all aspects of life, and not just in the overtly religious bits? By allowing the children to guide our initial theological reflections as we planned the service, and the secondary process of reflecting during the service itself, we had enabled them to articulate a 'gospel in the gospel' that was powerful for them, but also hugely relevant and challenging for everyone there.

You can follow up some of these ideas in:

Chapter 4: Engaging through the senses
Chapter 8: Children as theologians
Chapter 10: Engaging with one another.

8

Children as theologians

Theology for children in church

Earlier in the book we considered worshipping together as a way to ensure that we don't perpetuate the idea that learning is for children while worship is for adults: people of all ages learn, and all human beings have a capacity for worship, for encounter with the divine.

Preaching is almost always a place where worship and teaching/ learning meet. We learn *about* God at the same time as we get to *know* God better. Preaching is when we open up the word of God – the story of God's love for the world – so it's a vital part of how individuals and congregations are nourished on the journey of faith and discipleship.

Karl Barth, the renowned twentieth-century theologian, famously said that all his theological understanding could be summarized by a simple rhyme he learned from his mother: 'Jesus loves me, this I know, for the Bible tells me so.' But this didn't stop him writing 13 volumes of *Church Dogmatics*. The most important truths of the Christian faith  can be condensed into a few short sentences (as in the creeds), but scripture itself and the last two thousand years of Christian theology give us a rich and beautiful tradition of exploring simple truths in a myriad of ways.

Much of this wondering and exploring has found its ways into our liturgy – set prayers that have stood the test of time – and into hymns and songs. These often contain summaries of key aspects of the faith, using established turns of phrase and images that might need some unpacking, especially for those who are new to church or who are just starting to learn some of the more technical church language. That's one kind of theology that may need to take place in an all-age talk.

Sometimes we can do this by paraphrasing as we go along – so as to neither exclude nor patronize – using both the 'official' words and simpler words to say the same thing, as in this example from Ruth Harley:

> 'When we consider the mystery of the Incarnation, when we think about how amazing it is that God became human in Jesus ...'

Using short phrases can help here, by steering us away from long explanations that are no easier to understand than the thing we are explaining!

Sometimes it might mean exploring more deeply what we do and say in church, and why it matters – this might mean digging deeper ourselves into what we believe and how we tend to express what we believe.

'Jesus died to save us from our sins' is easy to say, but how would we explore what it means with children or an all-age group? What does this look like when done well?

- Try talking to someone you know from a church of a very different tradition. Do they understand it the same way as you? What ways have they used to explore it with all ages?

Another key aspect of theology that we will probably want to include in our all-age preaching is what our theology looks like *outside* church, taking into account that although your congregation have church in common, their lives during the rest of the week may be incredibly varied – work, school, home, leisure, travelling, community and so on are all contexts in which we can do theology outside church, if we're resourced well *in* church:

- What does it mean to do 'what Jesus would do' in the world (and the little corner of the world) we'll each be living in this coming week?
- What does it mean to love our neighbours as ourselves?
- What do we do when Christians disagree about what love is and what it looks like?
- How do we see God's love at work in the world and in our lives?
- How do we reconcile faith in a loving God with the suffering in the world?
- How do we live as people of Jesus Christ in the particular places we find ourselves each day: at school or nursery, at home and in the local community, in our workplaces and leisure activities?

Faith in God generates a lot of questions! Deep theological foundations, gained through immersion in scripture and worship, wider reading and conversation with fellow disciples, will enable our preaching to resource our congregations as they wrestle with these questions –that's how we and they will grow in faith. One of the challenges of preaching with all ages is to take the simple 'Sunday school' theology of God's love and explore it in a profound and life-giving way with people of different generations, who are seeking to live out that love in a rich variety of settings. Parents and grandparents may need resourcing as they try to share the faith with the next generation – encouraging 'faith at home' is one of the big challenges not only for Christianity but for other faiths too.

Theology by children

> Children can cope with much more complex ideas than people think. The most common mistake in all-age preaching is dumbing things down so much that it's no good for children, let alone adults.

Earlier we looked at what it means to hear the voices of children in church. But what do children say, once we start to listen? Can young children contribute theological and spiritual insights? What happens when you ask big questions of small people? What happens when small people ask big questions of you? We know from the testimony of scripture not only that Jesus put little children at the heart of his ministry and of the Kingdom of heaven, but also that God can and does speak through anyone and everyone, including children.[1] Opposite are some examples of theological thought collected from children in key stage one (age four to six).[2]

---

1 The most obvious example of this is the boy Samuel in the Temple, hearing the voice of God in the night and being commissioned to bring a difficult message to those in authority (1 Samuel 3).

2 Some of these are from my children, and some from other children I know. They have all given permission for their words to be shared here.

'Can we pray to God about my eczema? First I want to pray to God to take away my eczema. Then if God doesn't do that, I'll pray that it can be less itchy. Then if God doesn't do that, I'll pray that God will help me not scratch it. And then I'll say to God that we're not joking. Because we're not.' (age 4)

'It's important that we call God "Our Father" not "My Father" because we are all God's children together.' (age 5)

'God didn't make the world out of *nothing*, he made it out of *love*. Tell people that instead.' (age 6)

'In the circuit of love God is the battery, Jesus is the fuse (because the love of God comes through Jesus) and the people are the light bulbs.' (age 6)

'I think God is sort of outside time so that he can see the whole world and everything, he could even see it backwards if he wanted to.' (age 5)

'Did God actually save the Queen? Maybe the Queen was standing at the edge of a big cliff, and she was about to fall off the cliff, and God could reach out his hand and hold her hand so she didn't fall off the cliff. That would be saving the Queen. But God doesn't have a body, so he doesn't have a hand, so that wouldn't work. Maybe God would have to ask someone who did have a hand to go and hold the Queen's hand. But what if that person wasn't listening?' (age 5)

In a discussion about the Eucharist, and specifically about what the different bits of the service mean for us once we leave church at the end of the service, we wondered, 'How does what we do in church escape from the church at the end of the service?' We started with an outline of a church, and one child had drawn a big red heart on the altar.
Me: 'Tell me about this that you've drawn.'
Child: 'It's the prayers.'
Me: 'And how do the prayers escape from the church at the end of the service?'
Child: 'We carry people's needs around with us in our own blood.'
(age 5)

'Do you think cathedrals celebrate enough? I think they should smile more and dance about a bit. God is really fun and they should tell people … And they need to make you go wow and feel really small, in a kind of nice way.' (age 5)

'When I ask God things I wish he would just tell me the answer, but maybe he wants me to work some things out for myself.' (age 6)

The picture below is a reflection by my son, then aged 9, on the Good Samaritan, created in response to a sermon (for adults) that had suggested we see Christ most clearly when we're on our knees. He suggested that Jesus is like an image on a laptop with the screen tilted downwards 'because God is angled towards the earth'. He had noticed that in scripture it was the people at the lowest levels (literally and metaphorically) who were quickest to recognize who Jesus was. We see Jesus most clearly when we are with those he spent his time with.

The children who made all these comments used language and ideas they were familiar with to give voice to profound truths about God and humanity, and about God's relationship with us.

Whenever I read and reread these, and whenever I have a conversation like this with a child, I wonder whether we sometimes make our questions too easy, too trivial, too factual. Can we avoid the kind of language that excludes, while still raising our expectations of what children (and indeed adults) can think and feel? What better context for exploring deep questions could there be than a supportive community with the capacity to open up tough questions prayerfully and pastorally?[3]

> Over time, some of the children's naïve confidence will rub off, and it will smooth down some of the adults' doctrinal hackles … Some of the children's questions will stay around and create a climate in which some of the adults feel free to ask questions too.[4]

Children as preachers

My daughter preached for the first time when she was 11. It was an all-age Eucharist, with a baptism, in a neighbouring church where the curate had decided that all the roles that could possibly be done by someone who wasn't ordained would be done by children and young people.

She chose to preach about the idea of baptismal vocation and interacted with the congregation by getting them all to make themselves a badge bearing their name, and their first calling – to be a child of God. She then invited them to think about what it might mean for the baby being baptized, and for them, to live out the call to be a child of God who 'shines as a light in the world to the glory of God the Father' – and how they might encourage one another and the baby as he grew up. My daughter has been to a lot of baptisms – she used to come and help me with them. Her talk certainly drew on this experience but was very much her own work. She managed to communicate

---

3 For much more on this, see Rebecca Nye, *Children's Spirituality*, London: Church House Publishing, 2009.

4 Elizabeth J. Smith, 'Whose Prayer Will Make the Difference? Eucharistic Renewal and Liturgical Education', in David Holeton (ed.), *Our Thanks and Praise: The Eucharist in Anglicanism Today*, Toronto: Anglican Book Centre, 1998, pp. 99–114, p. 104.

something that connected with all the different generations in the church and left them something that would remind them of it when they got home.

Not all children would be comfortable preaching a whole sermon! But many have great ideas that are well worth sharing, and if we give them the resources and the opportunity their preaching can be good for everyone. The previous reflection chapter included an experience of enabling children to contribute 'micro-sermons' – this is something that most churches could replicate, with some forethought, courage and time.

- Can we and our children's work leaders/Sunday school teachers set aside quality time to work with the children on a particular Bible passage?
- How might we use discussion, art, drama and quiet reflection to enable the children to process the story and communicate their ideas?
- How might we enable the children to express their ideas during the service, either aloud or through artwork (projected or printed in the service sheet, or displayed around the church)?
- When children speak in church their voices are too often greeted with indulgent laughter or applause, which children experience as patronizing. How might we help the adults in our congregations to respond respectfully and appropriately to the contributions children make?

Flexible language

Small children's use of language is often more flexible than adults' – at least in spoken form.[5] Children – along with those new to faith – may also not have the official vocabulary to express key concepts in faith.

---

5 The current emphasis on grammar in primary school SATS seems, in my experience at least, to be associated first and foremost with written work.

This sometimes means that children will say the 'wrong' thing, or articulate theological ideas in ways that are idiosyncratic.

This can be a real gift. Where adults may be stuck with the theological clichés they've been taught over the years, children often have to put together their thoughts out of the language they have available in ways that can be poetic, challenging and refreshing.

> 'Heaven isn't up in space, it's everywhere, but differently real. It's full of people and hugs and love, but mostly love.' (age 5)

Non-verbal theology

Most of us probably think of theology as something that is expressed through words. *Theos* means 'God', but *logos* doesn't just mean 'word' in a literal sense, but something more like *the divine reasoning implicit in the cosmos, giving it order and meaning.* So theology isn't just 'words about God' but something much more interesting. My experience has been that it is possible to do theology without words at all.

Children, especially younger children, may have a unique gift to offer to a congregation, using play, art and interaction to express theology that adults and older children might reduce to words. Especially for those whose preferred spiritual style (see Chapter 6) isn't word-based, non-verbal means of engaging in theology, worship, prayer and communication can be liberating.

A two-year-old and I were playing in the vestry with the sand box normally used for extinguishing votive candles. He wanted a person, so we cut out a person shape from paper. He said, 'Go bed. Ill.' So we found another piece of paper for a blanket, and my toddler friend tucked him in. He then looked around, and found in the re-cycling bin an empty communion wine bottle. I picked up the bottle, mimed pouring a bit into the lid, and the toddler very gently helped his paper person sip from it. He then took the paper person out of his bed, and played with him actively again, as if he had recovered.

This story uses a few words, but the key communication was through action and play, allowing the toddler to communicate his capacity for empathy and some sense that the communion wine was restorative – being around in the vestry a lot, he knew what the wine was for. Or perhaps he was using it as a medicine bottle? Or both? His communication through actions rather than words drew my attention to the restorative and healing experience of the Eucharist – and reminded me of the times when I have brought communion to people who were sick, or even dying. His play opened up layers of meaning for me in a way that was intriguing and moving.

The following chapter reflects on a particular instance of this kind of non-verbal theology at work, in a situation in which even academic theology acknowledges that words may not be adequate to capturing and communicating theological truth: the Trinity.

9

Reflecting on the Trinity

Beforehand I prepared a strip cut from a bed sheet, approximately 8 to 10 inches wide and the whole length of the sheet. I made it into a loop, but put in three half twists, then glued the ends together – a loop with a twist is known as a Möbius strip, and they have some amazing mathematical properties.[1] I also brought with me scissors and a crayon.

I began with a question: 'How big is God? Isaiah wondered how to express his experience of God – when he wrote about his vision of God he said that the hem of God's robe filled the whole Temple. When we look up at the roof of the church, and when we look down at the hem of our own clothes we can get just a glimpse of what Isaiah felt.

'But God is bigger than that. God is bigger than we can possibly imagine. Mathematicians have a word for anything that is impossibly big: *infinity*.' Here we made the infinity symbol with the fabric.

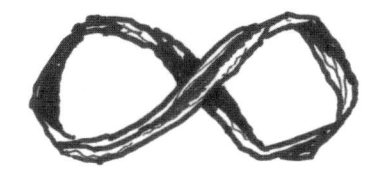

'Like a circle, you can trace it round and round with your finger – and it never stops, it has no ending. Even if we think of the biggest number we can, it's always possible to add one to it to make it bigger – infinity is different because we can't count to it, it's just impossibly big. God is infinite – bigger than any number could possibly be,

---

1 You can find out more about Möbius strips on the internet, if you want to try them at home. See, for example, http://en.wikipedia.org/wiki/M%C3%B6bius_strip.

and bigger and more awesome than we can ever really get our minds around, and we can't ever get to describing God completely, because if we think we have, we'd find that it wasn't God we were describing after all, but something less than God.'

I then revealed that there was something different about this loop of cloth. The twists make it into a Möbius strip, and we demonstrated one of its properties: it only has one side. We checked this by drawing a crayon line all the way along one side of the cloth, and finding when we got back to our starting point that both sides had been drawn on.

'Some things are just hard to get your head round! People sometimes are worried about how hard it is to get your head round God. How can God be one God, but still Father, Son and Holy Spirit? Three and one, all at the same time! But as we've just seen, even a bit of bed sheet can have both one side and two sides at the same time, so it's not surprising that God is more awesome and mysterious and interesting than that.'

I then explained that this Möbius strip actually has three twists, which means it can do another mysterious thing. The children helped me cut carefully along the length of the loop, guessing what we'd end up with: one loop? Two? In fact, what we end up with is one big loop, with a knot in it! And the knot is a bit special.

While I teased open the knot, and arranged the fabric, I asked the children to go round the congregation with the microphone, asking people to explain the Trinity using illustrations they'd heard. People suggested the shamrock (clover) leaf, water/ice/steam, sun/light/heat, and Jaffa cakes – chocolate/sponge/jelly! Together we all wondered about how these weren't quite right – they either divided God into parts or 'functions', but mostly they seemed to reduce God to something we can understand and get hold of. How can they really get to the heart of the mystery of the Trinity if God is infinite and our brains aren't?

By now I had finished arranging the fabric. A Möbius strip with three half twists, cut along its length, creates a perfect Celtic trefoil, which is one of the established 'pictures' that we have of the Trinity. At this point I felt I'd earned the round of applause that I received.

This is as far as I had planned – revealing the trefoil was going to be the climax of the talk.

That was when I realized the problem: this is still just a bed sheet doing a clever trick with 3D geometry. It doesn't tell us anything more about God than a shamrock leaf or a Jaffa cake. We can rearrange the cloth to remind us of all sorts of things about God that we already know: a tick to remind us that God is good, or a heart to remind us that God is love. So we did.

At this point I'd run out of ideas, but the children hadn't. They made the fabric back into a circle again, and then climbed into it. And then a wonderful thing happened – once inside the circle, the children all started hugging  each other and dancing. At this point I didn't feel there was much left to say.

Reflecting back, I wish that I could guarantee the same result if I used this idea again! Play is great at enabling creative thinking and encouraging wonder, but by its very nature we cannot fix the 'results'. We had experienced a moment where God had communicated through the children, teaching us something profound and wonderful about playfulness, mystery, community and ourselves in relation to God as Trinity. Such moments aren't ours to contrive, but we can allow ourselves to be open to them and hospitable to them. But had I chosen to end with the bed sheet trefoil as planned, we would have missed something wonderful.

I am sure there have been plenty of other occasions when we've missed an experience like this because I failed to spot it or didn't 'let go and let God'.

You can follow up some of these themes in:

Chapter 6: Engaging in different ways
Chapter 8: Children as theologians
Chapter 10: Engaging with one another
Encountering God again.

10

Engaging with one another

When my daughter first started learning the clarinet she could only play a handful of notes. My husband, who plays jazz piano, got her to play those few notes in a pattern, then improvised around them. I will never forget the look in her eyes as she heard her notes contributing to a whole new piece of music.[1]

Preaching with all ages asks something similar of us: when we value the contributions of everyone, even those who may only have something small and simple to say, we can help them see their contribution as part of something bigger. Sometimes they might provide a contribution around which we can enable everyone to improvise. This asks us to pay quality attention to what people are offering – their gifts and insights – as well as to their needs. It is also a gift we give to them, by offering them our genuine attention.

It also means enabling a genuine interaction. As preachers we can offer questions or thoughts that the congregation can respond to in a variety of ways:

- by suggesting ideas out loud that everyone can hear – this will probably need a roving microphone;
- by pondering/wondering to themselves;
- by drawing or writing something, individually or communally;

---

[1] To hear what this sounds like when it's done by phenomenal jazz musicians, listen to 'So what?' from Miles Davies' iconic album, *Kind of Blue*.

- by talking with one another, perhaps within a group seated close together, or deliberately with people they don't know so well – encouraging conversations during a talk provides an opportunity for younger and  older members of the congregation to listen to one another and learn from one another.

Any of these modes of interaction can be combined. It's worth thinking ahead (and signposting to the congregation) what sort of interaction will be used.

We must always make sure we give people time to think. This means asking our questions in such a way that if there's a pause or a silence, we don't feel we have to fill it straight away.

If we are wandering between groups in conversation, and we hear something amazing, we should always check with the person whether they'd like to offer it to the whole congregation or are happy for us to share it. If we're intending to read out or display what people have written or drawn, we should also be clear about this – people (including children) should have a sense of agency about what kinds of ideas they are happy to share in public.

Different ways of sharing ideas will suit different people – over time we work out what's going to work in our own setting. I've seen sticky notes, graffiti boards and even Twitter hashtags used to generate discussion during sermons!

The challenge of engaging with one another

In his book *Transforming Preaching*, David Heywood comments:

There is a spectrum as to the extent of congregational participation, depending on the amount of control you, as preacher, wish to retain. At one end of the spectrum is the typical 'family service' talk, in which most if not all of the questions are closed questions: that is, they have a right or wrong answer. At the other is Doug Pagitt's concept of 'progressional dialogue' in which the preacher starts the topic off and then follows where the congregation leads.[2]

I suspect he is right that the heart of the matter is the preacher's desire for control, and that closed questions probably *are* standard in many all-age talks.

Ruth Harley has helpfully distinguished between two kinds of question that we may use:

> 'We might sometimes think that children always need clear, repeatable answers, but my experience is that children are happy with not "knowing the answer", so long as they know that it's OK to not know. There are "knowing the answer" questions, and there are "wondering about" questions, and with the latter we are not trying to find an answer, we are thinking and exploring together to help us all understand more. When the children ask a question, I will often ask "Do you think that's a 'knowing the answer' question or a 'wondering about' question?" And when I'm preaching I will often say "this isn't a 'knowing the answer' question, it's a 'wondering about' question". I think having this framework has helped children and adults (including me) to understand what sort of conversations we are having when we discuss things, and what sort of space I am inviting them into when I preach.'
>
> *Ruth Harley*

2 David Heywood, *Transforming Preaching: The Sermon as a Channel for God's Word*, London: SPCK, 2013, pp. 140–1. The book he refers to is Doug Pagitt, *Preaching in the Inventive Age*, Minneapolis, MN: Sparkhouse Press, 2011 (which itself is an update of *Preaching Re-Imagined*, Grand Rapids, MI: Zondervan, 2005).

If we are to engage in theological conversation during preaching, then we need to be willing to ask both kinds of questions, and more:

- Questions to which we don't know the answer – we're seeking others' wisdom.
- Questions to which there's more than one answer – a breath of wisdom is good.
- Questions to which there's no knowable answer – much about God and life is mysterious and we won't ever run out of wondering.
- Questions that invite imagination and creative thinking – play can generate theology.
- Questions that invite a story – our story and God's story are intertwined.

Genuinely open questions give opportunities for members of the congregation to make real contributions, and all-age congregations are particularly able to do this because they have a greater breadth of experience and attitude to draw on, and from which all can benefit. But asking open questions is a matter of trust. Interaction and conversation in preaching is a public loss of control or, at least, a sharing of power.[3] We all need to ask ourselves, 'Do I trust my congregation? Do I trust the children in my congregation?'

Unhelpful contributions?

Asking the congregation for answers, questions, ideas and thoughts is often the thing we are most afraid of in all-age preaching. What if someone says something unexpected, unhelpful or off-topic? If we have charted the terrain thoroughly (see Chapter 2) we will probably

---

3 The idea that we can control what people will get out of *any* sermon is an illusion, but it's only in an interactive sermon that we discover this!

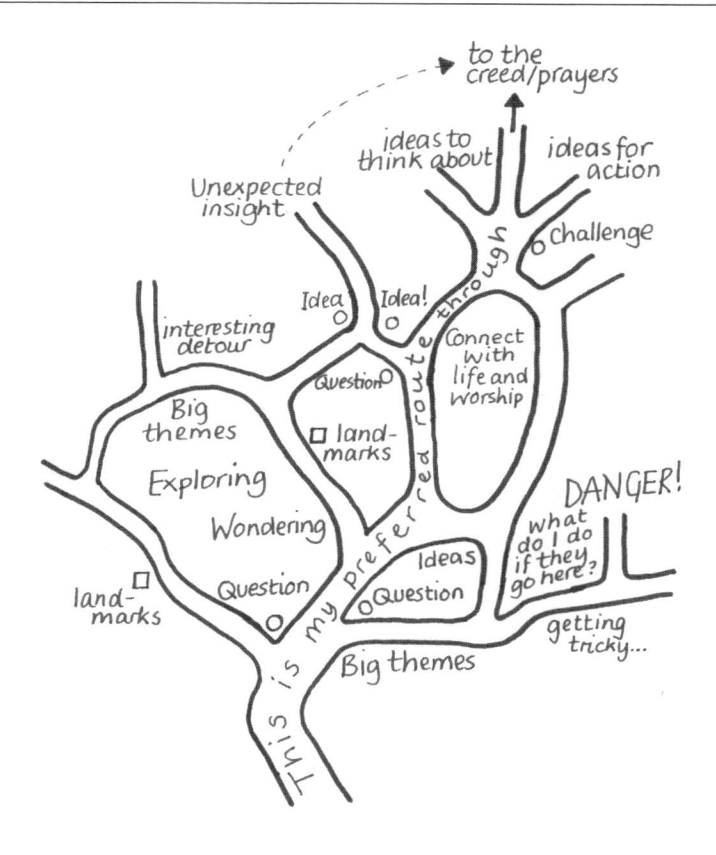

have seen some of the likely directions discussion might take already and have a plan for how to value those contributions. We might have a 'plan A' – our preferred route through to the creed and the prayers, or to the next song, but be aware of some likely detours. Some of those detours could easily be accommodated if they come up.

Remaining open to ideas, directions and insights that we simply hadn't thought of is also part of the process. Some of the most powerful moments in my own all-age talks have come directly from a member of the congregation – all I've done is not shut them down.

There are times, though, when a contribution heads off in directions that we don't think we can weave into the talk. Sometimes we can't follow up someone's idea because it would take too long, or need too much explanation. In these cases we can quite legitimately 'park' their idea for another occasion. If a suggestion really is off-topic or heading for a dangerous area, there are some ways we can head off an unhelpful diversion without discouraging the person who made it:

- 'That's an interesting thought – we might have to come back to that another day, because it's a really big idea.'
  (We can make a note to respond more fully later – how might we work with that person to plan how their idea could be explored further?)
- 'That sounds like something we might need to include in the prayers.'
  (We can make sure whoever is leading the intercessions is able to respond appropriately.)
- 'I'd never thought of it that way – can I ask you more about that after the service to make sure I've understood?'
  (We can get into the habit of encouraging conversation after the service.)
- 'I love that idea – can you draw me a picture of it and we'll show it to everyone at the end of the service?'
  (This can be useful if a child has an idea that's hard to explain, as it buys us time, perhaps during a song or hymn, to have a proper look at the picture with them and get a fuller explanation. The child can then share this with everyone later in the service if it feels right to do so.)
- 'Good thought – what other things can we add to that?'
  (This can be a helpful affirmation if we're aiming to get lots of different responses to follow up, and we might not have time for all of them.)

Shared activities

Interaction doesn't have to be limited to talking. Shared activities can be another way for a congregation to explore God's word creatively and interactively. Here are a few more simple ideas that can be used on a variety of occasions.

> 'My favourite all-age talks are the ones when we do something all together. My least favourite are the ones when just the children come to the front and someone talks and then asks us boring questions.' (age 11)

Paper chains

Preparing a paper-chain activity is easy with some double-sided sticky tape and a guillotine. Stick the tape along one of the long edges of each sheet of paper, leaving the backing on, and guillotine the sheets into strips so that there's a small square of tape at the end of each strip. A stash of pre-made strips can be used to gather contributions from the congregation that benefit from becoming a collective response rather than remaining individual: thanksgivings, gifts or talents being offered, pledges to action, and so on. I've used them on Vocations Sunday, All Saints, the Week of Prayer for Christian Unity, services for Scouting and Guiding groups, and other times when it felt right to reflect together on being the Body of Christ, diversity in unity, or working together.

I usually ask the congregation to construct the chain, which inevitably involves people interacting and working together. Depending on what I've asked them to write on their paper I might invite them to talk to the people around them about it as they do this. This can be a great way of making the medium match the method.

The end result is a colourful way of bringing together everyone's suggestions and contributions, which can be offered during the prayers, draped over the altar or pulpit, or displayed in some other way. I would usually aim to leave a paper chain in church (with a little notice explaining what it is about) for a while after the service when it was created – it's a reminder for those who were there, and a visible sign to visitors that there's all-age or children's ministry happening.

Wordles[4]

A wordle is a way of presenting a collection of words around a common theme. They can be created using various free online or downloadable tools, are highly configurable, and easy to make for anyone who is used to using a computer. This might be a good way to draw on the expertise of a teenager.

Before people arrive, put up a big graffiti board (or even just a flipchart) near the entrance, and have someone stand by it inviting people to contribute a single word on whatever your theme is. (When we did this in my church we were gathering one-word reflections on what it felt like to 'Come into the House of the Lord' as part of our celebration of the Presentation of Christ in the Temple, as told in Luke 2.22–40.) Most people will contribute a word if they understand what's being asked of them – and older children and adults can help the younger ones to write their words down. Duplicated words are fine – it's part of how the process works. At the same time, have someone there typing the words into a laptop.

---

4 See www.wordclouds.com or http://www.wordle.net, for example. They are also sometimes known as tag clouds. Make sure that you have practised beforehand so you're used to the process and have all the right plug-ins for your browser.

Then, once the service starts, whoever typed in the words can paste them into a wordle generator, to create from them a beautiful piece of art ready for the talk. It's worth thinking ahead about what sort of shape, colour and typeface you might want to use – these factors can communicate just as strongly as the words.

Given the right technology all this can be done 'live' in the church building, creating the worldle and projecting it during the talk. If not, it may be possible to print out some small versions ready to hand out during the talk. I have done it both ways. Projection is easier and quicker if you have everything set up, but printed versions can be taken home at the end of the service.

The talk itself can reflect on the content of the wordle, picking out some of the words and unpacking them a bit, letting them resonate with the life of the church and with scripture.

The lovely thing about wordles is that they honour every contribution – they can be set up to include all the words that were input – but they also honour the 'wisdom of the crowd' in that the more times a word is included, the bigger it appears in the final version. As a way of celebrating diversity and unity, individual and collective experience, it works really well.

Why not use the finished image in other ways? It could be included on an e-newsletter, on the church's social media accounts, and as a discussion starter for home groups.

I have used wordles in this way with school groups for an RE day in church, for a whole-church reflective process during Lent, and as a way of including the whole congregation in Mission Action Planning.

Shoeprints

This activity works well for any service reflecting on themes of journeys (whether actual or symbolic). I have used it during Lent and on All Saints' Sunday.

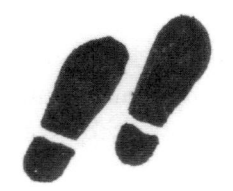

The activity requires a roll of wallpaper liner and several marker pens, and some willing volunteers to draw round people's feet as they arrive in church. I have previously used masking tape to stick the paper to the floor of the central aisle, and got people to have their feet drawn around just as they've reached the pew where they're going to sit. If people would like to have their feet drawn round more than once, they absolutely can!

By the time of the talk the paper should be nice and full of footprints. It's good if there are several different colours of pen as well as different sizes of foot.

During Lent when we used this activity, we invited anyone who wanted to take part to fill the footprints with words and pictures that reminded them of what it means to trust God, and how God cares for them day by day, as well as any worries that they wanted to bring to God – fears for the future. Not everyone was willing or able to get down low enough to write in the footprints, so we began with some conversations that allowed those less able to articulate their ideas for others to write.

On All Saints' Sunday we used this activity to reflect on the 'great cloud of witnesses' who had 'run the race' before us. We started with one another, giving thanks for the people around us in church who encourage us on our journey of faith, and then thought about the people who had shared the faith with us in the past, and then to modern saints who had inspired us, gradually working our way back to the saints of the early Church and to the time of Jesus (and indeed beyond!). We used the footprints to help us see ourselves in continuity with the whole Church, past, present and future.

Story books and story exchanges

For Bible Sunday an easy activity involves inviting the congregation to share the Bible stories and verses that have been most important to them. This can easily be done by handing out small pieces of paper and pens, and inviting everyone to write or draw the story, Bible passage or verse that they have chosen, and something about why it is important to them.

These can then be shared in a number of ways, involving different ways of interacting:

1   Invite people to swap papers with one another – this involves more personal interaction.
2   Collect all the papers and then invite people to take one – this is more anonymous.
3   Gather the papers and stick them into a scrap book – this creates a communal product.

Either way, the talk can carry on while people write, draw and interact, taking soundings from individuals who are happy to share their thoughts.

To make this activity more chaotic, people can be invited to make their paper into an aeroplane instead, and fly it to someone else in the church. I have done this once and it was great fun, but I wouldn't use it with all congregations. What it does do is provide a clear reminder that the word of God is for us to share, and that there can be a certain random, opportunistic quality to this.

There are more shared activities, particularly the creation of art-works, suggested in Chapter 12.

As with all activities, nobody should be forced to participate. The usual rule of thumb applies:

> With any activity, operate on the basis: **All may, some should, none must.**

Parallel activities

It can work well when we offer an activity that anyone can participate in if they wish, which is clearly and directly linked to what we are preaching about, but isn't necessarily for 'show and tell'. Examples might include:

- Giving pipe-cleaners or plasticine to the congregation and inviting them to make things in response to the talk.
- Inviting people to draw responses during the talk – doodle pads and pencils in the pews are standard in some churches, or people can be encouraged to draw on the notice sheet.

'For the Transfiguration, we offered "magic painting" (when you paint it with water the colours appear). I said near the start of the sermon that we were thinking about changing and being changed, and that anyone who wanted could do some magic painting while they were listening – many children and some adults did. During the sermon I linked what I was saying to the image of magic painting revealing what is already there, as the transfiguration revealed what is already there in Jesus. Towards the end I invited people to think about an experience of realizing something is different from what it seemed – the magic painting was one among several possible examples of this. Participating in the painting enhanced engagement with the themes we were wondering about together for those that did it, but without getting in the way of others' engagement.'

Ruth Harley

For more about how particular activities can enhance engagement in different ways, see Chapter 12.

11

Reflecting with stickers

I once gave an all-age talk at St Paul's Cathedral, at an anniversary service for the London taxi drivers' charity for disadvantaged children. I was told that there would be about 700 people there, of whom approximately one-third were 'the great and good', one-third were taxi drivers (many of whom were of another faith), and one-third children (some of whom might have additional needs).

I was given a choice about the reading, and I chose Matthew 25.31–40, the first part of the parable of the sheep and the goats. The 'gospel in the gospel' was that if we can start to see the King – Christ – in everyone, we become more like him, and find that in the Kingdom of God everyone matters, everyone is important. To that end, I had prepared 700 stickers, each with 'VIP' printed on them.

When it came to the service, I saw that the seating plan had been worked out in a way that meant that the three groups of people were largely confined to three different sections of the cathedral, which turned out to play into what I'd prepared.

First, we talked about how you know someone might be important – we noticed that some of the people at the service (the clergy) were wearing big gold cloaks, and others (the civic dignitaries) were wearing big gold chains and special hats, and others (the pearly kings and queens) had amazing costumes. I invited the taxi drivers to take the stickers and stick them on the VIPs – perhaps these people were the ones most like the King in the Bible reading? The civic dignitaries (complete with chains of office) all received VIP stickers.

We then dug a little deeper. I gave fresh stickers to the civic dignitaries and asked them to stick them on the people who might be 'these my children' – whom the Bible reading says we should treat as if they were the King himself. The children ended up with a VIP sticker each.

Finally, I gave more stickers to the children, and asked them to identify anyone left who was doing what the King asked, treating people as if they were a VIP. It didn't take long for all of the taxi drivers to end up with a VIP sticker.

The gospel in the gospel was simple: when we treat everyone as if they might be Jesus, the King, we become more like him, we learn to see ourselves and one another as he sees us, and we start to live as if the Kingdom of God was already here: a kingdom in which everyone matters, everyone is important, everyone is valued.

By this time it was a bit of a free for all. Almost everyone had got up out of their seat, interacted with people very different from themselves, and affirmed those people as important in the eyes of God. We had effectively acted out the heart of the parable, and in the process we had subverted the seating plan, which itself is a lovely bit of 'Kingdom theology'. The activity we did broke down the careful arrangement of the different groups of people and made everyone mix it up – the act of sticking the stickers on people meant that they had to cross what might have been invisible barriers, in a physical and embodied way.

I had been on a short placement at St Paul's Cathedral around 15 years before I did this talk, and the level of perfectionism and meticulous planning involved in worship there had scared me – I had only just started at theological college, and with my low level of competence and confidence at the time, St Paul's had felt like a place where any mistake would be a disaster. Preaching for this service, 15 years later, was the first time I had been back, and it was still scary.

I had planned something that would deliberately subvert all the things that I had learned about the cathedral on my placement, and I think I only realized during the actual service how much of a risk it was. There's a good reason why cathedrals tend to do things formally: the building is huge, the acoustic means you have to speak slowly and clearly, and there are huge numbers of people involved, logistically, to make everything work. By doing something that countered all of the usual ways that the cathedral worked, I was not only embracing the potential chaos myself, but also asking everyone else to do so as well. I hope the vergers have forgiven me by now …

As it turned out, what I planned did work – mostly. People were surprised to experience something so interactive – it wasn't what they were expecting. That, too, is in keeping with the nature of the parable, in which the usual hierarchies are turned on their heads and something of a new order emerges.

A challenge that I should have foreseen was that once everyone was moving around, it became much harder to speak and be heard, even with the excellent sound system. It was a little like a Christmas crib service – so many children milling around and enjoying themselves that the talk can barely be heard. Fortunately, the key message was communicated not in words but in actions.

One thing I learned for myself is that although it was me and my talk that generated the holy chaos and the interactivity, it was the cathedral's own hospitality that gave permission for it to happen, that offered its space so generously. The cathedral was out of its comfort zone, but willingly so. It reminded me that a huge part of St Paul's Cathedral's vocation is to be a place of hospitality for any number of organizations as they bring their work before God for prayer and blessing and celebration. Before I even arrived with my stickers, St Paul's had opened its doors to this wonderful, diverse congregation of people. Before I opened up the Gospel reading with them, they had already enacted it in real life, through the work of the charity itself. This realization was both reassuring (that I had simply articulated what was already true) and humbling (in that they had brought the gospel in the gospel with them – it was not something that *I* had given to *them*).

It was only much longer after the event that I started to question the activity itself. It had done what I had intended, and more, but with hindsight I realized that in involving everyone so actively I had left less scope for people to opt out if it was something they weren't comfortable with. Sticking stickers on each other isn't a threatening activity for most people, but there may have been some there for whom it was difficult, and the way that I had set it up meant that my usual rule of 'all may, some should, none must' was in jeopardy – I had left insufficient room for permission to be withheld. If I were to do the activity again, I would try to do it in such a way that it involved less actual contact and gave more scope for people's own agency. This might have been by encouraging people to offer each other stickers (or some other token) rather than to stick them on each other. This would, itself, have been a more congruent way of enacting the intrinsic value that each person has, and the respect that we owe one another.

You can follow up some of these themes in

Chapter 10: Engaging with one another
Chapter 18: Engaging with church life and mission.

12

Medium and message, process and product

Medium and message

Is it possible for our preaching to enable the kind of 'discipleship learning' that Jesus' own first disciples experienced? Their growth as disciples all took place in the context of personal encounter: from the Canaanite woman who took Jesus on in a debate over the scope of his ministry[1] to his threefold forgiveness of Peter on the beach after the resurrection,[2] Jesus taught in the context of relationship. Real, transformative meetings between the incarnate God and those he came to save, in which the approach Jesus used – using stories, questions, healing, everyday experiences, and living a life of love – was just as important as the content of his words. As preachers we – quite rightly – strive for the right words, but we must also embody what we preach. If we are to preach the gospel, we must live the gospel – even as we preach it.

Every approach to preaching has implicit values – theological values – and this book is at least in part about ensuring that our preaching flows from values that are in keeping with the Christian gospel and the Kingdom of God. These include:

---

1 Matthew 15.21–28.
2 John 21.

- Paying attention to the voices that don't usually get heard.
- Orientating ourselves towards transformation, reconciliation, wholeness.
- Valuing everyone.
- Working and learning together.
- Trusting God.
- Enjoying and caring for creation.

Rather than just stating these values when we preach, we enact them in the *ways* that we preach – the methods we use, the kinds of activities we share, the balance of silence and interaction, the risks we take, the materials we use. In a way, these are almost like extensions of our body language and tone of voice. Whenever we plan a talk, it's worthwhile asking ourselves: what are the theological values underpinning the *way* that I'm going to preach, and are these in keeping with the *content* of my talk? We might term this 'congruence' or even 'integrity' – it's about ensuring that the surface communication isn't being undermined by other, unintentional messages that we might not be aware we're sending, but that may well be picked up by members of the congregation, even if they're not sure why what we're saying isn't quite ringing true.

Feedback from colleagues and members of the congregation can often help us identify when this has worked really well and when it's not quite worked – they may also see things that we don't see, because their perspective is different, and this can be incredibly useful for our ongoing learning.

Much of this book explores how we draw on this understanding in our preaching. The following section builds on this, particularly reflecting on the relationship between the process we engage in and the sort of product that might emerge.

Process and product – making art together

In Chapter 4 we looked at some ways to use visual art in all-age preaching, and in Chapter 10 we looked at some simple communal activities. But what if we want to go further than looking at other people's art, and doing simple craft activities? Chapter 17 reflects on an experience in which my congregation accidentally created a communal art installation, beginning with the pre-schoolers' service and ultimately involving the whole congregation. This experience made me want to explore the possibility of setting out to create art together as a way of opening up God's word.

Churches are full of people who were told as children that they were no good at art, just as many people are told that they can't sing. Often the first stage of creating art in church is to persuade people that they are allowed to try, and that art isn't a forbidden place for them. For some people, contributing one small element to a larger piece of art feels safer than creating something on their own, and can be very empowering.

We see this in powerful works of contemporary art such as Anthony Gormley's *Field for the British Isles*,[3] which consists of 40,000 simple clay figures, made by school pupils in Merseyside, their families and other members of the local communities. A church probably can't attempt something on this scale, but the values that underpin this artwork are absolutely possible to live out in smaller-scale, temporary projects. Art can respond to and articulate the 'gospel in the gospel' for a particular time and place. Particularly in church buildings, displaying communal artwork on a temporary basis is much more

---

3 It is well worth reading the Arts Council educational resource accompanying this sculpture, which articulates the values that underpin the art. These are very much in keeping with the ethos of all-age preaching as I have sought to describe it in this book: www.artscouncilcollection.org.uk/sites/default/files/Field%20 for%20the%20British%20Isles%20-%20Education%20Information%20Pack. pdf.

likely to be practical and 'politically' acceptable! Here are some examples.

'During Thy Kingdom Come we had a large piece of artwork going on that everyone could contribute to. The picture evolved as a prayer of thanksgiving (as in the Benedicite) and was used at the Sunday service.'

Sue Milton

'During a Passiontide service we simply had a large outline of the cross and a pile of newspapers and magazines. With reflective music in the background we ripped the newspapers and magazines and made a collage of the cross. It ended up as a kind of montage of fragmented words and pictures.'

Susan Lucas

'We often create an altar frontal during the first part of the service, which is then brought forward at the offertory and used as the Eucharist is celebrated. Paint sticks are brilliant for this – and clean to use. A favourite was the one where we asked the congregation as they came in to draw around their hand and then we decorated all the hands as an expression of Teresa of Avila's prayer, "Christ has no body now on earth but yours".'

Carolynn Pritchard and Nicola Bown

'At the annual memorial service at Great Ormond Street, families were invited to contribute a petal with the name of the child they were remembering written on it, creating a giant, beautiful sunflower.'

Dorothy MB

One thing that emerges clearly from these examples is that creating a piece of communal art is likely to 'spill over' from the sermon slot into the rest of the worship, into church life generally or even into the whole local or gathered community – and that artwork created communally outside of a service can be completed and offered during worship. These pieces of art have connected with liturgy, mission, the local community, issues in the contemporary world, pastoral care and human experience, and can contribute to a broader and more integrated experience of the Church as the Body of Christ, uniting those who might never meet each other.

For these sorts of projects to work requires integration of children's ministry, worship planning, preaching and missional activity, as well as good communication on a practical level about use of space and resources, and how the finished product will be used or displayed. These are all factors that may require (as well as contribute to) the sort of cultural change alluded to in the Introduction.

Another feature of these examples is that their value is in the process of their creation as well as (or more than) in the final end product. Preaching with all ages, in the way that I have described it in this book, is very much about process, just as a sacrament is more about action than about object: we *share* and *eat* the bread and we *pour out* and *drink* the wine, we *pour* the water at baptism and we *pour* or *smear* the oil, we *give* the lighted candle … The 'things' we use alongside our words in preaching have a sacramental quality – they are not just objects but are invitations to action, to engagement in a process, and towards transformation.

In a society that values measurable outcomes very highly, prioritizing process over product is counter-cultural. Sometimes the process does not result in a product at all – or at least not one that is tangible or visible. Some communal activities, such as that described in Chapter 7, are very tangible and visible during the process itself, but don't result in an 'item' that can be displayed – there may be nothing for a 'show and tell'.

Try this:

Next time you're in church but not responsible for leading the service, try doodling on a notice sheet or even on the service sheet if it's single-use. What do you notice?

Doodling sets us free to think creatively without having to produce a 'finished product' – and can give us insight into our own thought processes.

As you plan an all-age activity, ask yourself:

Does this activity need to produce something that can be displayed or used?

A process-focused activity can, of course, produce beautiful and powerful products. The creation of a piece of communal art involves encounter with God and with others, and something of this encounter often shines out of whatever is produced. The prayers and thoughts and questions that go into the creation of the art somehow linger in the paint and fabric and paper and glue, and in the images and textures that have been put together.

Try this:

Write the name of someone you want to pray for on a piece of paper in big, beautiful letters. As you pray for them, start to decorate around their name – use colours if you like. Add more to the image each day during your prayers. At the end of a week you will have made something that is beautiful not just because it is art but because it is prayer.

As you plan an all-age activity, ask yourself:

Is what I'm planning to be done by individuals and then put together at the end, or will the process be collaborative throughout? This might be a practical question based on the layout of your building and the size of your congregation, or it might be determined by the gospel in the gospel.

Will the medium/process be something that everyone can join

in with? Does it require a skill that the congregation can teach to one another as part of the process?

There is a relationship between the particular process we engage with (or the artistic medium we use) and the sorts of insights that are generated. The paint, plasticine, wool or fabric (or whatever we are using) becomes another 'variable' in our approach to exploring the gospel in the gospel. Some media encourage quick, energetic thinking, while others ask us to slow down and focus. Reflecting with plasticine is different from reflecting with stones. The medium you choose will become a 'given' and givens are gifts because limiting the range of choices gives us parameters within which to exercise our freedom and imagination. Limitations are, paradoxically, liberating, especially when we want to encourage creativity.

Try this:
Read through a Bible passage several times – choose one that you're going to preach about. The first time, build something out of Lego as you read. Then next time play with plasticine. The third time use scissors to cut up paper into shapes. The fourth time play with some natural objects such as seeds or stones. What do you end up making? What changes in the way that you think about the scripture? What does each 'creation' offer to your reflections?

Ask yourself:
If we're going to display or use what we make, will it be just during the service, or have a longer life? Does the intended use affect what materials and media we can use? Will it need to dry (or bake, or cool down) before we can use it? How does the medium fit the theological themes we're exploring?

Finally, if you are creating something that others who weren't involved in its creation will see and wonder about, it's worth thinking through how to enable this also to be a fruitful part of the process.

Try this:

Show someone else what you made in the exercise above, and ask them to describe it or respond to it. What connections do they make based on your Lego, plasticine, paper, other creations?

Ask yourself:

Will the item invite them to add a contribution or response, or trigger a reflective process or prayer? What might you need to do to help people engage with what's been made? Can you introduce it to people without over-explaining it?

13

Reflecting on scripture

For this talk I began with a washing line (held at each end by two tall people), clothes pegs and a lot of pictures[1] of Bible stories. I included in my set of pictures some that were very much 'illustrations' of specific stories, and some that were more oblique, even abstract or symbolic. I included a mixture of old masters, cartoons, modern art, images from different cultures around the world, and children's drawings, as well as images from the Lego and Minecraft Bibles. This enabled a range of people within the congregation to be able to claim expertise, and prevented those with a theological education holding all the power. I had also included some images that could have represented several different stories: water, fire, stones, bread, a woman with a baby, a tree, some grapes … In the activity, these were the most hotly contested images, and were a really great way of helping people see some of the patterns and recurring themes in scripture.

The pictures were left in the pews before the service, and during the sermon I invited everyone to find a picture and bring it to the washing line and peg it in what might be the right sort of place to create a picture-Bible – starting with creation on the left and ending with Revelation/heaven on the right. The task (as I had hoped) generated a lot of conversation, interaction and sharing of wisdom and questions, both within family groups and between people of different generations who might not usually have a conversation.

---

1 When I first did this activity in an all-age service, I prepared a large number of images, downloaded from the internet and laminated.

Once we were happy with our washing-line Bible, we looked at it together and asked ourselves: if this was a song with lots of verses, how would the chorus go? What words would we want to include in the chorus that go with the stories that make up the big story of the whole Bible?

Reflecting back, I think the thing I was most excited about was the quality and generosity of the conversations that took place. The task was slightly trickier than I had anticipated, so that it took everyone's ingenuity to work out a solution that we were all happy with, and to start to see patterns and themes emerging. The question about the verses and chorus of the song was something that had occurred to me on the spur of the moment. We happened to have a singer-songwriter in the congregation who had occasionally written songs based on things I had said in sermons, and I think I must have caught his eye as we were drawing to a close with the activity – we never did write the song, but the question did help us start to think about the 'big story' of scripture.

I also realized that the activity had taken longer than I'd antici-pated. It was sufficiently active and engaging that it didn't feel long at the time, but it prompted me to be more aware of the need to keep the overall length of the service manageable for families. Each church will have its own conventions about the ideal length for a sermon, or for an all-age talk, and it's usually good to work within these conventions, though if an activity takes off, and everyone is fully engaged with it, it can often be allowed to run longer without people becoming impatient.

oOoOo

When I subsequently used this activity in a teaching session for trainee ministers, I learned something completely different – this time about myself. I had invited them to begin with a chronological arrangement, as before, but then to look for other ways to group the images, hoping that they would identify themes that would help them in their reflective work. There were some great suggestions for other ways that we could use the images creatively to help us reflect. But what challenged me most was the student who pointed out, 'There are almost no difficult bits of the Bible here – where's the judgement?' This was at least partly because I'd originally created the picture resource for use in all-age worship, but it made me wonder about whether my idea of a suitable 'refrain' for the Bible is honest enough about the complexity of scripture, and warned me against the temptation of heading always for those parts of scripture that I find inspiring and encouraging, or particularly formative in my life of faith.

> **You can follow up some of these themes in:**
>
> Chapter 4: Engaging through the senses
> Chapter 6: Engaging in different ways
> Chapter 10: Engaging with one another.

14

Engaging with scripture

Choices

When we are presented with a piece of scripture to preach on that we find difficult, a passage that makes us ask 'Where's the good news in this?', using the ecological model (Chapter 2) can sometimes help us find a way to explore something unpromising, and we may even end up feeling that this was a gift after all – the grit in the oyster shell that helps us grow a pearl.

But there are probably times when we may need to look at changing, or perhaps shortening, a reading when we have all ages worshipping together. This isn't because we need to hide the Bible's darker side,[1] but because there usually isn't time in the context of all-age worship to unpack adequately a really difficult passage of scripture – some bits of the Bible really do require that we wrestle with them all night until they yield their blessing.[2]

Looking at my own 'washing line' of scriptural pictures reminded me that I, just like the compilers of the lectionary my church used, have made decisions about what to include and what to miss out. Some of the pictures I had included represented stories that had shaped my own growth in faith and journey as a disciple of Jesus.

---

1 If you are in any doubt that it has a darker side, look again at the story of David and Bathsheba (2 Samuel 11) or Jael (Judges 4).

2 The story of Jacob wrestling with the angel is in Genesis 32.

> What passages of scripture have helped you know God and yourself better, challenged you at crucial moments, and seen you through tough times? Why are they important to you? How have you explored them?

Stories that shape us

There are also 'go to' Bible passages that have proved themselves to be so foundational for the Church and Christian life that we (or our church) may decide to prioritize exploring them with the congregation. For God's people in the Hebrew scriptures, the stories of the Exodus and then the Exile were so formative that they were repeated again and again in different ways. What stories continue to shape the Christian Church's self-understanding? What stories and other passages of scripture help us learn what it means to be the people of God? In addition to the obvious stories that form the cornerstones of Christian doctrine (creation, the stories of Jesus' birth, death and resurrection), a list might include:

- The parable of the prodigal son.
  God's love for us, God's forgiveness, and our identity as God's children.
- Psalm 23.
  God's enduring presence through hardship, and the promise of an eternal home.
- The Beatitudes.
  What it means to live faithfully and prophetically in the world.
- Jesus teaching his disciples to pray.
  A pattern of praise, intercession, forgiveness and aligning ourselves with God's Kingdom.
- Jesus' teaching on the Summary of the Law, and the parable of the good Samaritan.
  Our call freely to give and receive care, and to challenge our own prejudices.

- The manna in the wilderness.
  God's faithfulness and our dependence.
- 1 Corinthians chapter 12.
  Diversity in unity in the Church, and valuing diverse gifts.
- 1 Corinthians chapter 13.
  Love as the motivation for all our action, and which lasts for ever.
- The accounts of the Last Supper, including the washing of feet.
  Community and loving service, and our commitment to 'do this in remembrance' of Jesus.
- The Great Commission.
  The command to continue Christ's earthly work.

What would you include in your own list of 'key passages' for your church, and for your congregation in their journey of faith (both together and individually)?	How might you use each of these in all-age preaching?

All these are passages that we can engage with again and again, going deeper each time, adding new insights from new people, places and situations. One encounter with the story of the prodigal son, for instance, will not yield all the possible wisdom and insight that the passage has to offer.

Different perspectives

The washing-line activity in the previous chapter reminded me how much I tend to use images – particularly multiple images from different artists and different cultural traditions – to help me understand scripture more deeply.

When I was compiling my Bible picture resource I intentionally set out to gather a diverse range of images. We can do the same with other sources of insight, by reading commentaries that look at scripture from particular perspectives that are different from our own.[3] Learning what others have seen in a passage reminds us both that we are in continuity with a long tradition of biblical interpretation and that what others see will be shaped by their contexts, just as our own observations are. Sometimes we need to look at scripture, and indeed at Jesus, from a completely different angle.[4]

Context

Another piece of learning that I took from the Bible washing-line activity was the way in which the individual stories relate to the whole. A short passage is part of a chapter that is part of a book, and the writer and editors who wrote and compiled it will have had an idea in their minds about how that one passage relates to its immediate and wider context in the Bible. It's always worth reading the chapters either side of the text we're preaching on, and looking at the overall message and shape of a biblical book to see how our bit fits in and what it contributes. The sorts of questions we might ask ourselves include:

- How does 1 Corinthians 12 (the body and its members) help with St Paul's overall message to the church in Corinth?
- Why did John include the wedding at Cana and the feeding of the five thousand so prominently in his Gospel?

---

3 One book I have found especially helpful if I'm not sure where to start is Ernesto Cardenal's *The Gospel in Solentiname* (New York: Orbis Books, [1976] 2010), a book of transcribed conversations from a small group of Nicaraguan revolutionaries in the 1970s. What I love about it is that their perspective is so different from my own, because their life experience is so different from mine.

4 USPG and the Methodist Church have jointly produced two excellent picture resources, offering a range of images from global Christianity: *The Christ we Share*, London: The Church Mission Society/Methodist Publishing/Us, 2004; and *Born Among Us*, London: Methodist Publishing/Us, 2003.

A good biblical commentary is helpful here.

The Bible is a collection of books, in a range of different genres and with different purposes. Each book emerged at a particular time and place. Knowing what kind of thing we are reading helps us understand what it is saying.

- Am I reading a record of a historical event? A parable? A poem? Something else?
- When I read an epistle, for whom was it written, and what need was it addressing?

The washing-line activity invites the congregation to look at the whole of the Bible, and wonder whether there is one, big, overarching story – and if so, what that story might be. That big story has to be able to 'hold' all the small stories, and the small stories must somehow contribute to the big story. It should be possible to 'bounce' between the small scale and the large scale as we interpret scripture:

- How does this story contribute to or challenge my understanding of the overall story of God's relationship with the world?
- How does my understanding of the overall scriptural witness to God's relationship with the world help me interpret this particular passage?

If you make your own set of picture cards, try this exercise:

- Turn all the images face down and turn over two.
- You're not looking for a matching pair, but for some insight that that combination of images offers.
- Do they have something in common, or do they tell us very different things about God? Is one of them more inviting or intriguing?
- Do you feel a more personal connection to one of the stories/ images than the other?

In the light of my own learning above, I am more aware than I was of the danger of looking at scripture and seeing what I want or expect to see. Using the exercise above in a small group, or working with a group of friends or colleagues to create the picture resource in the first place, opens us up to different perspectives and so broadens our own outlook.

Key themes

The washing-line activity also drew out some key themes. The question, 'If these stories were all verses of a very long song, what would the refrain be like?' invited the congregation to consider the deeper themes both in the overarching story of the Bible and in individual stories. Here are some key themes – what more would you want to include?

- God's promises and purposes through the generations.
- God's self-revelation to the world.
- Social justice and worship.
- Reversals – the first and last, the strong and weak, etc.
- Conflict and reconciliation.
- Sin and forgiveness.
- Vocation, identity and purpose.
- Suffering and restoration.
- Living well in the world with one another.

Scripture also draws on recurring images. This became clear as I compiled my Bible picture resource. I included a picture of a woman with a baby – was that Mary? Elizabeth? Hannah? Sarah? Was the stone the one that David used to kill Goliath, or the one that Jesus didn't turn to bread, or the one not thrown at the woman caught in adultery? These recurring images can help us to make connections within the Bible and reflect on the deeper themes that they are exploring.

Here are some to start with. Use the right-hand column to suggest others, and then fill each box with a note of the places in scripture where these themes are explored.

Bread	Journeys	
Stones	Water	
Light and darkness	Farming, gardens and vineyards	
The natural world and its diversity	Banquets, feasts, eating and drinking	

15

Reflecting on the Eucharist

In my previous church, and in my theological college, we held an occasional 'teaching Eucharist' at which we would admit any children who had been preparing to receive communion for the first time.

In a teaching Eucharist there is no sermon or talk, but instead a 'reflective commentary' running through the service with some simple activities, gentle conversation and times of 'wondering' to help the congregation experience the Eucharist more deeply.

We aimed to pick a different occasion in the church year each time, so that the commentary could explore different aspects of the Eucharist:

- When we held the service at Pentecost, the commentary focused on the role of the Holy Spirit in worship generally and in the Eucharist in particular.
- On the Sunday after Ascension, we focused on how the Body of Christ is both Jesus' physical body and St Paul's description of the Church.
- Earlier in Eastertide we focused on Christ's presence in the community of faith.

We were able to explore how the Bible is woven into the Eucharist and where some of our best loved prayers in the service had come from, such as the 'crumbs under your table' (Matthew 15.27) and 'peace be with you' (John 20.19).

One of the challenges of preaching in this way is that the Eucharist has its own flow, and the aim of the reflective commentary is to help people engage with it, rather than disrupt it. We chose carefully which points in the service would be appropriate for a reflection, and when we need to let the normal order of things run. We identified a list of possible moments for a reflection, from which we would choose a different combination each time:

- Just after the opening greeting, reflecting on what it means to gather as God's people, and introducing the confession.
- Just before the readings, reflecting on the role of scripture in worship and our continuity with the community of faith through the ages.
- Just after the Gospel reading, drawing on particular themes associated with the occasion and relating them to the Eucharist.
- Introducing the creed, with particular attention to what we were learning that day about God and our relationship with God.
- Introducing the intercessions.
- Introducing the Peace, which would then flow uninterrupted into the Eucharistic Prayer.
- Before the final blessing and dismissal, drawing the threads together, and pointing to how what we had experienced might be lived out during the week.

Depending on the occasion and the particular themes we were exploring, we would pick one or two moments for a longer or more active reflection, and maybe two or three more for something shorter to help with continuity. We almost always had some form of reflection at the gathering and dismissal.

oOoOo

One of the tensions in this kind of service is that it draws attention to the possibility of worshipping and learning at the same time. Can our learning be worshipful? Can worship help us learn? Are there parts of the service that simply can't be interspersed with commentary? We found that the very part of the service that might most need to be explored was the part we didn't want to interrupt! By learning from each experience we developed some ways to address this issue:

- We started to weave reflection on receiving communion into other parts of the service. This helped us see the service as a whole, rather than looking at it in sections.
- We reproduced in the service booklet some of the artwork and comments/questions generated by the children during their preparation sessions. As people were waiting to go up to the altar rail they were able to use the children's insights in their own time of reflection.

We also found over time that it would be easy to overload the service with activity, so we identified a range of ways in which the reflections might be done, but didn't use them all in the same service:

- blank areas of the service sheet (and pens) for doodling;
- simple communal activities such as making a paper chain to reflect on gathering as God's people (see Chapter 10);

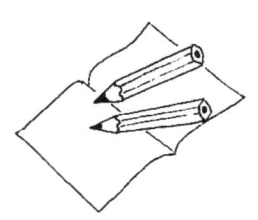

- a simple version of the ribbon activity described in Chapter 5 as an introduction to the confession and absolution;
- creating a temporary altar frontal (see Chapter 12);
- a question about personal experience to ponder alone or quietly with others;
- learning about something factual – such as where some of the prayers in the service

come from and how that can deepen our understanding;

- testimony from some of the children being admitted to communion, or from others in the congregation, about what receiving communion means – or means to them.

You can follow up some of these themes in:

Chapter 6: Engaging in different ways
Chapter 10: Engaging with one another
Chapter 14: Engaging with scripture.

16

Engaging with liturgy and worship

> The whole service preaches, and preaching can be both worshipful and sacramental.

Preaching takes place in an act of worship. If the whole service can contribute to the preaching, and the preaching is to be a worshipful encounter with God, this requires a level of interplay between the talk and the other elements of the service, which in turn invites collaboration between all those involved in planning and leading the worship in order to enable a holistic, integrated experience.

We can be alert to:

- Anything associated with the season or occasion that might shape our approach to the reading(s) as we discern the gospel in the gospel. For instance, the season of Epiphany explores God's self-revelation in Jesus – is this a helpful parameter to shape our thinking?
- Particular words or phrases from any set prayers in the service that might give us a nudge towards a particular theme or idea. I found the phrase 'heaven touching earth' (from the Church of England's additional collect for Christmas Day) especially rich in helping me explore the mystery of the Incarnation.

There may even be occasions when we want to scatter the talk through the service rather than having it all at once, as in the teaching

Eucharist (Chapter 15). A holistic approach to all-age worship planning can help ensure that the talk doesn't feel like a stand-alone event, but rather as utterly integral to the whole. When we start to plan, we can consider how the whole act of worship, from the moment people walk up to the church door until they get home again or even beyond, can open up the gospel in the gospel.

- How will music and song play a part? Songs can connect learning to worship, and we often remember what we have sung far better than what we have said or heard (see Chapter 4).
- How might the scripture and its key themes be worked into the gathering, at the introduction to the confession or creed, into the intercessions, the sharing of the Peace or the dismissal?
- How might any objects or actions from the talk become part of the prayers?
- What might be distributed at the dismissal and taken home at the end?
- How might the 'tags' between sections of an act of worship allow the gospel in the gospel to bring out the shape of the liturgy?

Redeeming the creed and integrating the prayers

I sometimes wish the talk could lead directly into the prayers. It can seem jarring to switch register from an engaging, prayerful talk to standing up and shuffling service sheets in order to say the creed or affirmation of faith. But shouldn't the creed feel like a completely natural bridge between opening up God's word and bringing the needs of the world to God? As we move from preaching into prayer, there is always something of this dynamic. We can bring all the concerns of our hearts to God precisely because God is God, and it is the creed that reminds us that we are encountering the Creator of the universe, who loved us into being and who loves the world enough to be nailed to it – this is the God we come to know through opening up the word, and who is going to hear our prayers. The creed can sometimes feel as if it is *about* God, but it, too, is an expression of our relationship *with* the God we encounter every time we worship, and who holds us even when we aren't aware of it.

If we worry that the creed feels like an intrusion, we can work on letting it emerge from the end of the talk as a route into prayer – and we can think beforehand about which of the authorized versions of the creed (most denominations have several forms) will best enable this to happen.[1]

Recurring themes and symbols

In some traditions that are very focused on the Eucharist it's absolutely normal for preaching to reference the Eucharist, or focus on an aspect of the Eucharist as a pivot between the ministry of the word and the ministry of the sacrament. It's good to think through what connections will make sense to our own congregation, as well as making sure we include those who receive a blessing as well as those who receive the bread and wine.

In churches that are not so Eucharist-focused, it's worth reflecting on what the formative symbols and themes are for the congregation. Baptism may be a much more significant formative symbol, or the Bible may be the central focus, or the cross itself. The gathering of the people and the sharing of fellowship might be at the heart of the church's self-understanding, or a particular social outreach project (and the values that

---

1 In the Church of England these are all provided in *New Patterns for Worship*, London: Church House Publishing, 2002.

underpin it) may be shaping how the church sees itself in relation to God and to the world.

> What is it that gives your church its sense of meaning and identity? How might you reflect this and explore it more deeply in your all-age preaching?

Something to take away

When we preach we hope that something of what we preach about will be remembered, and even make a difference to people in the coming days and weeks. Worship itself has a trajectory not only towards encounter with God but towards the dismissal as we are sent out into the world (where God is also already at work).

We can work with whoever is leading the service to help the gospel in the gospel 'escape' from the church and get out into the world, perhaps by means of something to take away – whether that's an idea, an item or a suggested action.

This might helpfully occupy the slot otherwise taken by the traditional 'show and tell' (when children's groups would present to the rest of the congregation what they have done). It can become an opportunity for people, if they wish, to articulate something that they would like to take with them into their daily life. If your church gives out the notices just before the final blessing, it might even sometimes be possible to connect the events going on in the life of the church and the community with the gospel in the gospel.

17

Reflecting on the stones

It was Palm Sunday, and Easter was late enough that there was genuine spring warmth in the air. In the morning Eucharist we had heard the version of the story in which the religious leaders tell Jesus that he must make his followers be quiet, and he replies: 'If these were silent, the stones would shout out.'[1] Later in the service we had read the Passion Gospel with different voices taking each of the parts in the drama, while the children had reflective activities using a floor mat version of the *Way of Life* sculpture from Ely Cathedral,[2] which was a familiar image to most of the congregation. It had been a good, but quite demanding, service, and at the start of a busy Holy Week I had not had much time to prepare for the afternoon 'Stepping Stones' service for younger children and their accompanying adults.

The line about the stones from the morning Gospel kept coming into my mind. I found myself wondering what the stones would have said, had they been given a chance. What would they have witnessed during their thousands of years on the surface of the earth, and what would they have testified as Jesus rode by on the donkey? I didn't get much

Come to him, a living stone, though rejected by mortals yet chosen and precious in God's sight, and like living stones, let yourselves be built into a spiritual house, to be a holy priesthood, to offer spiritual sacrifices acceptable to God through Jesus Christ.
(1 Peter 2.4–5)

---

1 Luke 19.40.
2 http://jonathanclarke.co.uk/commissions/ely-cathedral/.

further by the time of the afternoon service, but since I felt drawn to the stones, it seemed like a good starting point.

As it happens, as a church we were towards the end of a long and complex building programme, the working title for which was 'The Living Stones Project'.

The church extension had been designed as a resource for the church, the local community and visitors, providing hospitality, welcome and a place to have a drink and go to the loo. The church is a historically significant building, so permission for this project had been hard won: the stones from the north wall had been painstakingly removed, cleaned and stacked into a cairn by some of the women from the congregation so they could be reused to clad the extension, making the new blend seamlessly with the old. The building project was being overseen, and indeed carried out, largely by members of the congregation – we were blessed with a small cohort of energetic and gifted engineers, former military and others, who built almost the whole thing with their bare hands.

All this was in my mind, as well as the name of the children's service (Stepping Stones), and the way that we always used stones with the children's names on them in the gathering rite. No wonder the stones from the Palm Sunday reading that morning attracted my attention.

As the families arrived for the service I led them round to the place where the building work had been taking place. We looked together at all the stones on the ground: different shapes and sizes, some were carved and shaped, others were lumpy or broken. There were even some pieces of old concrete mixed in too. I invited the families to pick up some of the stones so that we could bring them into church. Children really enjoy picking through building sites, and their parents and grandparents were happy to join in. There was much laughter and thoughtfulness, and many interesting questions.

'How old are these stones?'
'How old is the church then?'
'What makes the stones smooth?'

'How did this stone get broken?'
'Did a dinosaur pee on this stone?'

By the time we had carried our armfuls of stones to the church door, we felt like we had started to form a relationship with them – they were no longer just objects. We put the stones down on the flagstones outside the porch, and went and got a couple of washing-up bowls full of warm soapy water, and some towels.

Washing the stones turned out to be just as much fun and just as thought-provoking as collecting them. I saw the stones being treated with gentleness, care and delight, as children and adults alike scrubbed and wiped and laid out the stones to dry in the sunshine. It reminded me of the woman with the ointment, or even Christ himself washing his disciples' feet.

I guided our questions to the Palm Sunday reading.

'What kind of story might the stones have told?'
'What would those stones have seen and heard?'

When the stones were clean, we brought them into church and laid them out on the chancel carpet. Our usual liturgy at Stepping Stones involved singing 'He's got the whole world in his hands', naming each child as they brought forward a stone with their name written on it, and putting the stones in a basket at the front. Today, that gathering liturgy felt even more apt.

This was already further than I'd got in terms of planning – already exploring the theme of stones and stories had helped the families engage not only with the scripture of the day and the liturgical season, but also with something in the wider life of the church. But with a chancel full of stones, lying higgledy piggledy on the carpet, yet seeming so special and significant, there inevitably came the question,

'What are we going to do with them now?'

I can't remember who it was who suggested that we go back to the

Ely Cathedral *Way of Life* sculpture. It has a striking and memorable shape, which had become well known in the diocese. Some of the children had encountered it at school, as well as during the morning service that day. They called it the 'wobbly cross' and suggested that we could use the stones to make our own wobbly cross – so we did. It ended up about 12 feet long, occupying a large proportion of the chancel, but leaving enough room either side to get to the altar and back.

As we arranged the stones in their new shape, I told the children some of the stories of stones in the Bible – we wondered together about the stones that Jesus hadn't turned to bread, and the stones that built the Temple, and the stones that had been put in the river on the way to the promised land. We looked at the shape we had made, and thought about Jesus' journey to the cross, and all the stones that were on the ground along the way. We wondered at the twists and turns in Jesus' journey and in our own. We thought about what the various stones in the story of salvation had witnessed, and what they would say, particularly about Jesus.

At the end of our service we didn't have the heart to clear it up, so we left it, thinking someone would complain that it was a trip hazard. Nobody did. So the stones stayed there all through Holy Week. We covered it with tiny candles during the Tenebrae service. On Good Friday the Walk of Witness ended by gathering around it. Then on Easter Sunday my seven-year-old scoured the churchyard for dandelions and filled every crack between the stones with what, by the 10.30 a.m. Eucharist, looked like tiny sunshines.

Reflecting back, several things stand out for me about this experience, which I found personally transformative. I am still learning from it.

I realized how important it is to listen to the silent ones, to create space for and empower those who don't usually get a seat at the table or whose wisdom isn't valued. The silent stones turned out to have a lot to say, just as the children's insights were a gift to the whole church. I found myself asking some questions:

- Who doesn't get heard in our church and in our local community?
- Whose stories are being lost or unvalued? How might we listen better?
- Are we learning to pay attention to children and take them seriously?
- What helps or hinders our ability to do this?

The experience also made me wonder about how children (or other minority groups) in my church were empowered to make decisions, affect policy, contribute to the development of strategies and take part in mission.

This experience showed how children can often handle symbols really well. The stones in this case were an amazing symbolic gateway into scripture, enabling us to connect the lectionary reading with the life of Christ, and even with other biblical stones and the roles they play in salvation history. I found myself wondering how we might explore more deeply some of the key symbols and themes and stories of the faith, particularly in worship.

It helped that stones were already part of the symbolic language of the church community as a whole. I was reminded again that children's ministry can be utterly integrated with the life of the whole church, and with the themes and symbols that are shaping the discipleship and vocation of the adults.

More widely it made me wonder whether we might be able to do more in the church to encourage a sense of holy playfulness and creativity among the whole congregation. We had accidentally made an art installation – next time, could we do it intentionally? What might be the place of symbol and art in our life together? Were there other prevailing metaphors and symbols in our church, and do all churches have their own, based on their own context, story and experiences?

It was also a real joy to lead the children and adults through a complex time of the Church's year, enabling them to contribute creatively in the way that the church lived through Holy Week. What we did with the stones was artistic, it was scriptural, it was devotional and it was liturgical. I'd go as far as to say that it was sacramental. And although it started as something that we did at Stepping Stones it became integral to the whole church's journey. It was particularly moving to see how the nature of the stone installation evolved through the week, and how different people and gatherings had contributed to that development. This reassured me that we, as Stepping Stones, had created something, but that we had genuinely offered it to everyone, and invited them to participate in it. It became something that we *all* owned or, rather, something that God owned and was sharing with us all.

Finally, I became aware that as well as hearing silent voices, we had, accidentally, done something really rather empowering for the children and for that Stepping Stones congregation. Our stone installation had occupied the chancel in a challenging way, inviting questions about the use of the space, to whom that space belonged, and how we might help all-age congregations engage with the idea of sacred places and sacred times (see Chapter 18).

Clearly, this sustained experience was the product of a particular combination of circumstances – it is an effective case study for how the model in Chapter 2 for finding the gospel in the gospel actually works, even if we haven't planned it that way! Although this particular activity may not be one that would naturally arise in every church, I hope it will encourage us all to be attentive to the stories, symbols and themes that are converging in our own setting.

You can follow up some of these themes in:

Chapter 4: Engaging through the senses
Chapter 8: Children as theologians
Chapter 10: Engaging with one another
Chapter 18: Engaging with church life and mission.

18

Engaging with church life and mission

Preaching in context

Right at the start of this book I suggested that an all-age talk is best planned in the light of its context in worship, in the life of the church and in the world. It's never just an isolated event, but can resonate with, contribute to and respond to the church's strategic vision and governance, especially in relation to mission, outreach and discipleship, and the way that the church community relates to the building itself and its location.

Space and territory

Church buildings are complex places. If they are historically signifi-cant it may be hard to change the layout or the seating, and the strong sense of 'sacred space' also means that certain parts of the building (particularly around the altar) may be perceived by all, or by some, to be out of bounds for anyone who doesn't have to be there to lead worship. Research has shown that in more formal churches even the congregation's unwritten 'seating plan' differentiates between people according to their level of expertise in participating in the service.[1] Boundaries between the different zones in the church may be marked by physical barriers such as steps or screens or doorways, or may be invisible but no less real.

Worshipping with all ages is already likely to transgress some of these boundaries, especially if an all-age service attracts a different combination of people from other services; habitual seating patterns may be (helpfully) disrupted if children and families are encouraged to sit near the front where they can see.

Preaching with all ages can be a helpful way to transgress and manage boundaries generously and gently, teaching in an enacted way about how the church building works, what the various zones are for and what they mean to people. As we preach we can enable children, families and newcomers to venture into areas of the building that should feel open to them, contributing to the process of a church coming to accept its intergenerational identity.

- When and how might your preaching involve moving (yourself, the children or anyone in the congregation who would like to follow you) to different parts of the building, such as the font, the altar or the pulpit?
- How might you help children to experience these areas of the church as particularly 'holy ground'? What stories might you tell there? Involving the children in the ministry that usually happens in those areas can help them to get a sense of their significance.

---

1 The research in question is in a paper by Sam Peters, who found that in a particular church those who knew all the right places to sit, stand and kneel and could perform all the liturgical gestures sat nearest the front, while newcomers who did not yet have that level of expertise, and young families who, for practical reasons, might not be able always to conform to the norms of behaviour were seated at the back, which was less exposing for them and less distracting for the 'experts' at the front.

- How might you show by your own words, tone of voice and body language that you are somewhere special, somewhere holy? Children learn from noticing what we do, probably more than from what we say.

My experience has been that when we trust children in sharing our holy things and places, modelling a sense of awe and wonder, they often respond well. It helps if our holy things and places have their own gravitas, too, and if we draw attention to this in the way that we approach them and talk about them if we are introducing them to children during a talk:

- 'Look how this stone step is so worn and smooth. I wonder how many feet have trodden here on their way to the altar. How amazing that your feet get to make it even smoother. See how gently you can tread on the step as you follow me.'
- 'See the water in the font – how it reflects the light from the windows. It's so pure and clean. I wonder if you were baptized in water just like this, in this font? Very gently, and one at a time, you can reach in and touch the surface of the water with your finger tip. See the ripples like circles.'
- 'This is a chalice, it's made from silver. Feel how heavy it is! It's very precious, because it's the cup we use for the wine at communion. Jesus also shared wine with his friends, and said to them, "This is my blood, poured out for you. Do this to remember me."'
- 'See how tall the candle is! We need to be careful around candles: stand far enough away that you can see how the flame flickers and changes colours, and the smoke rising up. This candle is special. We get a new one every year at Easter, and it reminds us that light is stronger than darkness, love is stronger than hate, and life is stronger than death.'

Sometimes it can be helpful to do something more daring with the church building, but I have often found when I've done this that I was in some way responding to an implicit invitation to do so. In

Chapter 11 I reflected on the way that I thought I had subverted the space in St Paul's Cathedral, but realized after the event that I had been responding to the hospitality that the cathedral had been offering all along. In Chapter 17 I reflected on the Holy Week installation that the Stepping Stones children had created in the chancel, which transgressed boundaries in terms of the use of that particular space outside of the usual time of their service. The chancel belonged to the children for an hour or so one Sunday a month, so allowing them to have a stake in its use for the most important week of the church calendar was a daring escalation of their agency in the church, but we couldn't have done it if the space had previously been completely out of bounds.

> How is your church laid out? Are any parts of the building inaccessible (because of either physical barriers, such as steps or screens, or invisible barriers to do with their particular significance) to particular groups in the congregation? Are any parts of the building unsafe? Who 'owns' particular spaces and determines how they may be used and by whom? Think through the impact that these boundaries might have (positively or negatively) in worship and on preaching.

Belonging and ministry

During Lent in my previous church we used to put up lists of all the rotas and church roles, so that people could amend the list if they wanted to stop doing one thing and try something new. This was timed during Lent so that the lists would be ready for everyone to be thanked and commissioned at the annual church meeting. The Lent after we started regular all-age worship, without any prompting, the children all signed up to join rotas – even things like joining the Parochial Church Council. It made us realize that we were becoming an intergenerational church, and that we could reflect this in all areas of church life.

Later, when I asked my children what it meant really to belong to a church, they replied:

> 'You know it's your church and you belong there because your name's on a rota. They know your name, and they miss you if you're not there.' (age 9 and 11)

Clearly there's more to membership of a church than being on a rota. But these two examples illustrate how powerful it is for children to make a real contribution to the life of the church and for a rota to demonstrate that they are known (by name) and valued. The majority of adults in full-time Christian ministry can recall a formative experience from their childhood in which they were empowered in a ministry role, from singing in a choir to helping with Sunday school, and from helping with welcoming and giving out service sheets to bell-ringing.[2] What they recalled most powerfully was a sense that they were being taken seriously and making a real contribution to the life of the church. Most of the roles that they fulfilled were within intergenerational teams in which they were able to learn by example and, in turn, help to mentor those who followed afterwards.

Just as the church building has visible and invisible barriers, roles within the church community and worship can also be tightly boundaried. Just as you might help children to move reverently into a particularly 'holy' part of the building, you can also help them move reverently into a particularly boundaried role. This might be by encouraging and resourcing children to prepare micro-sermons (as in Chapter 7) or it might simply be by giving children the opportunity to articulate their questions and ideas as we open up God's word

---

2 These were the findings of a piece of informal research I undertook on 'children as ministers' in 2015. I also heard many stories of people being disempowered, sidelined and ignored – experiences that were just as formative, but in much less constructive ways. My own experience of church as a child was dominated by not being allowed to sing in the choir because I was a girl.

together so that the congregation learns to hear that God's wisdom and praise can come 'out of the mouths of babes'.[3]

Common shared symbols

Preaching can also resonate with the Church's common shared symbols, not only those that are common to most churches because they shape our liturgy and are central to our faith (see Chapter 16), but also those that are specific to your own church. In Chapter 17, I explored the power of stones as a formative symbol for my own church: stones had already taken on a range of meanings in that place, connecting the past, present and future, and enabling the provision of hospitality on the journey of life and faith.

Think about whether your church has a particular symbol or guiding metaphor that is significant to the congregation or to the local community, and whether it's a symbol that the children in your church would be aware of and familiar with. It might come from an aspect of the church's architecture, its name or dedication, its location or its history, or from a particular tradition that has become beloved over the years. Symbols may resonate in scripture and theological tradition, including in liturgy, worship, hymns and songs, and might be fruitfully explored through art and creativity.

Faith in community and faith at home

As an all-age preacher we may have part of a person's attention for perhaps 15 minutes once a month. This isn't a lot of time to contribute to their journey of discipleship, but there are some things we can include in our talk that may help it last longer than the few minutes we're given:

---

3 Psalm 8.

- **Conversation**: opportunities for people to talk about things that matter, perhaps over a shared activity, so they can learn from and encourage each other – this learning and encouragement may well continue long after the talk is over, especially if it allows people across the generations to build friendships within the church community.

- **Take-home items**: something to take away as a reminder of 'the gospel in the gospel'. This might be an object, or a little card with a few words on it to stick on the fridge. The Church of England's *Life Events* team has produced some lovely 'giveaway' items for baptism services, and many denominations offer similar items especially

> A baptism all-age talk idea from Sandra Millar involves giving away baby socks to everyone to prompt thanksgiving and prayer.[3]

at Christmas. We can use these as they are, when appropriate, and let them inspire us to produce similar items for other occasions.

- **Something to do**: an action to do during the week, either alone or as a family, that helps us remember and live out the gospel message.

- **An idea**: something they didn't know before – a skill, an idea, ideally presented in such a way that they will remember it, perhaps when they encounter it again in another context.

Looking out and drawing in

If the church has an e-newsletter, social media accounts or some other way of sharing what's happening   more widely, we can offer to write up a little summary of our talk, its take-home message, or just a simple 'thought' from it relating to everyday life, so that it can be shared with those who were there as a reminder, and with those who weren't as a way of keeping in touch.

---

4 See https://churchsupporthub.org/idea/baby-socks-shoes.

> 'We used Facebook to share an Advent Calendar and 'Lent Challenge' activities, sometimes devised by our youth group, so that families could respond by sharing photographs of themselves participating in the suggested activities.'
>
> *Ruth Harley*

Translating an experience in church into something that communicates outside of that service is itself a theological and missional activity. Who might we work with to do this? How might the perspective of children or others who were there help us to work out what to say to the wider world?

Can anything produced in the service make its way outside physically, as well as virtually on social media? Could anything be left in the porch, if it's somewhere people will pass by? What about on a noticeboard by the road? Were there take-home activities or items that are intended to be displayed? How might they generate conversation?

How might we learn from people who are relatively new to our all-age congregation? Something drew them to church, and something made them stay. It's worth asking what works for them and what doesn't, particularly in relation to preaching. What ideas do they have for making it even better?

Chapter 20 picks up these themes, particularly in relation to preaching and pastoral care, and how preaching with all ages can contribute to the church's response to local, national and international events.

oOoOo

When we start to empower children in worship and in preaching, to hear their voices, to enjoy and value their contributions and to learn from them, we will find that there's a knock-on effect: we will need to reflect that same sense of agency and value in all areas of church life and mission. This is one of the ways that preaching with all ages can both reflect and contribute towards cultural change in a church that is seeking to become actively intergenerational.

19

Reflecting on Pentecost

It was Pentecost, and I had been invited as a guest preacher to a church in London: a 'normal' sermon at the early, more formal service, and then an all-age sermon at the later more informal Eucharist, at which there would also be children admitted to Holy Communion. I didn't know the church at all, or anyone there, so I had no prior relationship with the people to enable me to gauge what they might bring to the service in terms of gifts, needs and expectations.

Previously in my own church I had used bubble mixture as a way of understanding the relationship between the Holy Spirit and the Church: without air, the bubble mixture cannot be what it is meant to be – it is just mess, with no form. But with air inside it, it becomes the beautiful bubbles it was meant to be. At the same time, without the bubble mixture, the air is invisible, and we find it hard to understand its power, and may even forget it exists. In the same way, when the Holy Spirit fills the Church (and individuals) we become more fully who God created us to be, and in turn we reveal the reality of God's Spirit, active and at work in people, in churches and in the world. Armed with this idea, and having reflected at length on the scripture readings for the day, I approached the occasion in reasonable confidence that something would come to me.

The night before Pentecost, there was a terrorist attack on London Bridge. I followed events as they emerged overnight, and by early on Sunday morning, as I set off on the train to London, the details were becoming clear. There was nothing I could do for those caught up in it, but my preaching that day might need to meet a significant pastoral need for the congregation – there is always a pastoral element to preaching, but in this case it would be much more immediate. I wondered whether I should step aside so their own parish priest could be the one to speak? And I wondered about whether bubble mixture might be too frivolous for what I imagined might be a sober atmosphere.

About half the congregation arrived at church not having heard the news, so there was genuine shock as people gathered, comforted one another and shared information. I found some words for the first sermon that somehow seemed to hit the spot. But the all-age talk felt more difficult still. How do you bring together grief, shock, anger and fear, with the joy and excitement of Pentecost and admission to communion, when you have a congregation of all ages?

I began simply by encouraging the congregation to take a moment and breathe in and then breathe out a few times, to help us all (myself included) to be calm. As we breathed slowly, I reminded them, speaking softly as if I was leading a meditation:

'Jesus breathed the Holy Spirit on his disciples,[1] saying "Peace be with you", when he first appeared to them in the upper room, alive again.

'When we breathe in air, it goes to our muscles, right to the tips of our fingers and toes, enabling us to move; it goes to our brains, enabling us to think; and we breathe it out again and it carries our words into the world.

'Imagine that Jesus is breathing his Spirit and his peace into this church, and that when we breathe in we are breathing in the Spirit and peace of Jesus Christ. The Holy Spirit, and that gift of peace, goes to our bodies, to our muscles, empowering and inspiring our actions; to our brains, our minds, to inspire our thoughts; and when we speak, our words are words of peace, breathing out the gifts of the Holy Spirit in all our interactions.

'When we breathe in the Holy Spirit we are sent to think and act and speak as God's holy people for God's needy world. St Paul

1 John 20.19.

said the Church is the Body of Christ – and as we begin to receive communion "we are what we eat" and become more fully members of that body. If that's the case, then the Holy Spirit is the breath in that body, who makes the body come alive.'

At that point I got out the bubble mixture and offered the illustration that I had prepared. It had previously always generated great excitement, but on this day it didn't feel frivolous at all: there was more thoughtfulness, more calm and more concentration. I invited the children to blow bubbles (slowly for big ones, more quickly for small ones) as a way of 'rehearsing' the action of making something beautiful to be sent out into the world. As they did so, we wondered together about how our thoughts  and words and actions at our most difficult times might share God's gift of peace with the world.

Reflecting back, I realized that it was both risky and appropriate not to have prepared something fully scripted. Sometimes on tricky occasions it can be useful to have decided on the precise words that will communicate what needs to be said – I've always found this on Remembrance Day, for instance. But the particular situation that day, and my own level of uncertainty about how the congregation would feel and how they might respond, meant that I had no real confidence in my own ability to get it right. A script might make me *feel* in control, but it was no guarantee that I had, in fact, found the right words.

I was also very aware of being a stranger coming into their space when they must already have been feeling vulnerable. Not only was it harder than usual to trust myself, but it was harder to trust the congregation too – it didn't feel fair to expect them to generate lots of ideas.

I was left with trusting God, and trusting that my primary desire to care for the people as best I could, meeting them where they were, would enable me not to get in God's way. I think subconsciously this is why I chose to begin with the breathing activity, as I hoped it would put us all (myself included) in touch with the movement of the Holy Spirit among us.

You can follow up some of these themes in:

Chapter 4: Engaging through the senses
Chapter 20: Engaging with human experience.

20

Engaging with human experience

Preaching and pastoral care – a holistic response

The experience I outlined in Chapter 19 reminded me that when we are preaching, leading worship or preparing intercessions, we do so in the context of the world and its events, both large and small, joyful and heartbreaking. Church doesn't happen in a vacuum, the events of the world impact the people who are attending church – if only that they will want to respond in prayer – and a church must be able to offer hospitality to lament as well as to joy, to the stuff of life as well as to the stuff of faith.

The world that God loves is beautiful but very, very broken, and our worship and preaching has to be able to make room for difficult things in the world around us – there is nothing that we cannot bring to God for wisdom and in prayer. If we preach often, it's likely that at some point we will have to preach in the aftermath of a really significant event. Assurance of #thoughtsandprayers may not meet people where they are, particularly if there is a lot of anger, and it can be hard to find the right words.

All churches should consider putting together an integrated major incident plan that includes:

- Practical responses – which may be about use of the building and resources, if the incident is local, and immediate material needs.

- Pastoral responses – care and support for those affected, especially if they have a personal connection with the incident.
- Spiritual responses – how the church might express its care in worship, liturgy, the use of the church for quiet reflection and candle lighting etc.
- Political responses – how the church might contribute to transformation, reconciliation and justice, in keeping with the values of God's Kingdom.

Preaching is a small but significant part of this bigger picture: in the immediate aftermath of a major incident, members of the congregation may look to the preacher for comfort and for some way of making sense of what's happened. Parents may especially be looking for ways to explain to their children what's happened.

- Try not to overinterpret what's happened if the details are still emerging – it may not be clear if the incident is an accident or an act of terror, or if a particular person or institution will be found to be at fault.
- Find good sources of child-friendly explanations. The BBC (*Newsround*/CBBC) often produce resources quickly following major incidents, and www.assemblies.org.uk/ produces 'rapid response' assemblies that could be adapted for all-age use.[1]
- Focus on caring for the people in church that day. What are their needs, and how can they be empowered to meet the needs of others?

---

1 The site is searchable in case an archive resource is useful in a new situation.

In the light of what's happened, what does it mean for us (adults and children) to love our neighbour? What are the fundamental *values* that need to shape our responses as more details emerge?

- Sometimes people just need space to grieve and bring the complexity of their emotions. It may be appropriate to do away with the talk altogether and instead have an extended time of prayer – ideally with some prayer stations or activities that children can engage with. Would the person leading the intercessions be open to this? Remember, the psalms teach us that we can bring the whole range of human emotion before God.
- It is worth double-checking the readings and hymns/songs for anything that could be really jarring or particularly unhelpful; it can be helpful to talk through with a colleague if we can about how we might deal with these. We may be able to encourage a joined-up response in our church.

An incident needn't make the national news for it to have an impact on your congregation. Local tragedies are just as significant for the people they affect. A member of the congregation may bring their own particular sorrow or pain into church, and it may sometimes be appropriate to honour that and respond to it in the way that we worship and open up the word of God that day – we should always check with the person most closely affected as to how they want to handle this.

Difficult subjects

When a TV drama or documentary deals with a particularly difficult 'issue' there is generally an announcement at the end along the lines of 'If you have been affected by the issues in this programme, please do contact . .', with a telephone number or website provided. Should we be prepared to offer the same?

As preachers, we can be sensitive about how difficult topics are raised. Some Bible stories, especially those that deal with illness, death, disability or violence, can trigger intense emotions in people for whom the story resonates with their life experience. We should treat every such story as if it might belong to someone in our congregation.

- The church's own calendar or lectionary sometimes gives us something that will be hard to face and painful to explore.[2] Beginning a talk with an acknowledgement that it's not an easy subject can give those for whom it may be painful time to prepare themselves. Some occasions that generate a complex range of emotions are also generally considered especially suitable for all ages, such as Mothering Sunday.[3]
- We might not know whether a particular issue affects someone in our congregation, so we should always assume that there might be someone there who could be hurt, and work out how we will care for such a person in the way that we preach.
- If we think our talk (or the whole service's theme) might be difficult for some people, it's worth assigning someone who is pastorally skilled to keep an eye open for anyone struggling.
- All this is as true of children as it is for any other member of the congregation; when a child is in need of pastoral care we may well have to offer that care via the family.[4]

---

2 I am still not sure about whether it's a good idea to explore the story of Abraham's near-sacrifice of Isaac in an all-age setting.

3 Christmas can also be a time that triggers great sadness in people, particularly if people they love have died or are far away. The imagery around Christmas can be particularly hard for parents who have suffered miscarriage or the perinatal death of a child.

4 It is good practice for all those who preach to have a DBS check, and undertake safeguarding training regularly. If as a preacher we become concerned about a child, it may be appropriate to take those concerns to the church's safeguarding officer for advice.

Human and secular calendars

The Church has its own calendar, and parts of that intersect with the other calendars that shape our life experience, such as the school year and (in some communities) the agricultural year. Parts of it almost fit, but don't quite, such as the way that society's celebration of Christmas coincides almost exactly with the Church's marking of Advent.

Individual lives and family life have their own calendars, too – rites of passage, milestones marking significant changes, and times of celebration and loss may all be marked in church, and many of them can be reflected in all-age preaching.

Many churches hold an annual all-age service at the start of September to which the children bring their (new) schoolbags for a blessing. This often uses a luggage label with words of blessing or reassurance on it, which can be attached to the bag for the school year. In some churches the blessing is extended to any adults who want to bring a handbag or briefcase.

A baptism is almost always an all-age occasion. When it takes place in a main service, there is an opportunity in the talk to affirm the dual 'ownership' of the event: it marks the first step in an amazing journey that will last a lifetime, and as such is both deeply personal to the child and their family and significant for the church family as a time to welcome their newest member and to be reminded of their own baptismal identity.

When we preach on an occasion marking a moment in a human calendar, it helps if we have an idea of what meanings that occasion has for the people involved.

- What are the children feeling at the start of the new year? How might you go about finding out?
- Is your social context affluent enough that the children all get a new schoolbag each year, or not? Is the gospel in the gospel different because of this? What might an appropriate *practical* response be?

- Have you been involved in the baptism preparation, so that you can bring into the talk something of what the event means to the child (if they are old enough to articulate this in any way) and their parents?
- How might you empower the baptism family, their guests, and the regular congregation to discern together a gospel message that they can all share?

Life patterns

Ordinary life experience and smaller milestones can also be reflected in preaching with all ages. When we do this, it's particularly important not to make assumptions about the shape of people's families, or identity. Congregations include a wide range of different-shaped families, and not everyone who comes to an all-age service does so as part of a family group.

Community events

If our church is involved in community festivals and events, we'll need to pick up on the themes and underlying values that are being celebrated. How do they resonate with the gospel? How might our preaching draw on and contribute to activities taking place outside church?

> Our village festival was on the theme of superheroes. We had a stall on the Saturday and had a board up where people could vote for their favourite biblical superhero – the winning hero became the theme for the open-air service the next day. We had to do a pretty quick bit of planning that evening, but people loved the feeling that they could help decide what we did!

Many charities also produce excellent resources to raise awareness of issues such as homelessness, mental health and disability.[5]

---

5 There is a list here, www.jointpublicissues.org.uk/whats-new/the-public-issues-calendar/, including the dates when these issues are often (or officially) recognized in UK churches.

Particularly for themes that resonate locally or with our own congregation, it's worth looking well ahead and planning how preaching might contribute to the way our church engages.

Shared cultural references

Often different age groups operate with very different frames of reference – children, young people and adults probably don't all watch the same TV shows and films, or read the same books, or play the same games; some will go to work, some to school, others spend most days at home, some may travel a lot. It's worth avoiding examples that reflect the life experience and frame of reference for only one part of the congregation. We should use shared experiences if we can, or apply what we're saying to a range of contexts so that everyone in the congregation feels like we've noticed that they are there and care about their lives.

Sometimes a cultural reference has enough shared familiarity that you can use it in a talk with little explanation, or it is simple enough to be explained for those who are not familiar with it. The *Toy Story* movies, for instance, with their themes of loyalty and belonging, have inspired many all-age talks, and are (at the time I am writing this book) well known – but they may not remain so. In 2012 the UK had two cultural references that almost everyone in a congregation would grasp: the Queen's jubilee and the London Olympic Games. Both generated much reflection that went beyond the monarchy and the world of sport, and started to explore deeper values around identity, community, endeavour and faithfulness. Both also generated related activities that involved all generations. But both are now several years ago – they no longer offer the same recognition and familiarity.

Again, it's well worth working with the church's leadership team about local, national and international events, issues and celebrations, and how these might be marked in church.

21

Reflecting on creation

As part of our celebration of 'a season of creation' (September and October) I wanted a way for our service for younger children, parents and grandparents to reflect on the wonder of creation – not just of the 'finished product' of creation, but the process of creation. The aim was to explore together the idea that part of the way in which we are in the image of God is to share in God's creativity.

We began by teaching one another how to make pom-poms, just using 'pineapple ring' shaped discs of card and scraps of green and blue wool. As we started to wind the wool scraps around the rings, we read Genesis 1, slowly, pausing regularly to talk about each of the days and sharing what we found most amazing about the world, our experiences of looking up at the stars and the moon, the places we had been to, the animals and the plants that we found most interesting and beautiful.

Several things emerged from this process, some of which I had hoped for, and others that were fruitful in surprising ways.

First, we found that the act of learning how to make pom-poms encouraged interaction between the generations. The grandparent generation turned out to be the most experienced and were able to show the process to the younger members of the congregation, while towards the end of winding the wool around, the hole in the middle was so small that it needed the smaller fingers of children to complete the work. That each member of the group had something to contribute enabled us to enjoy a communal creative process.

Second, we found, as I had hoped, not only that our conversations about God's creativity were supported by our own creativity, but that we paid attention simultaneously to God's work and to our own. And we found that the physical engagement with the materials in our hands meant that we became more emotionally engaged with what we were making. In this, we learned something about the relationship between Creator and creation.

Third, because we were using scraps of a variety of different blue and green wools, rather than specially bought whole balls of wool, not only were we drawing on the contributions of other members of the wider church congregation who had offered odds and ends, but also there was something powerful about using scraps and making something beautiful and new out of what might otherwise have been wasted. This, in turn, led us to reflect on the key theme of creation season, that of treasuring and cherishing the earth and its resources.

Fourth, we found that when we reached the moment when the winding stage was complete, and it was time to cut around the layers of wool, tie up the middle and remove the card rings, it felt like a real risk, a moment that could destroy what we had done if we got it wrong. We had the experience of looking at our wonderful creation, full of potential, and knowing that in order for it to be what it was made to be, we had to take that risk. And that we wouldn't find out exactly what it would be like until we did. Would the emerging patterns of blue and green be as we had hoped? What might be surprising? We talked together about how this felt. We talked about the parts of the world that made us frustrated or sad or anxious. It was this that led us into prayer: we held our pom-poms in our hands as we prayed, noticing that each of them was different and unique (and that some were neat and plump while others were a little ragged, but held just as gently and lovingly). As we prayed, we sang, softly, 'He's got the whole world in his hands'.

oOoOo

Reflecting back on this experience, I also identified some wider theological themes and sources that could be drawn on should we revisit the same activity and scripture again. Scripturally, I found resonances in the psalms, and especially Psalm 8, which reflects beautifully and profoundly on the relationship between God, creation and humanity, and which places value on the voices of children in expressing this relationship appropriately through praise and worship. This helpfully connected wonder at God's creation, praise of the Creator, and human responsibility with the created order.

I found myself drawn to Julian of Norwich's vision of God's love as a 'little thing, the size of a hazel nut' in the palm of her hand, which was 'all that is made' and which 'lasts and will last for ever because God loves it'.[1] As an image it captures both the overwhelming scale of God in relation to the created order, and the love and care that God shows to his creation. It is at once mysterious and intimate, profound and ordinary.

Both of these additional texts proved to speak powerfully to a wide range of congregations, from schools to ecumenical outdoor events, particularly when combined with some kind of sensory (visual, tactile), creative and interactive means of engaging. On various occasions these included (in addition to a reprise of the pom-pom activity): 'unveiling' conkers from their shells and holding them, paying attention to their beauty and uniqueness; writing prayers for the world on a papier mâché sphere and passing it round; rolling balls of multicoloured plasticine in our hands, and so on. We found, as Julian's *Revelations* suggested, that our reflections were made more intense and engaging, and communicated best, when they were done through the combination of words and embodied activity. We also found that when we undertook creative activity together, as a community diverse in age, gender, personality and life experience, we gained insight into our nature as human beings created in the image of the trinitarian God.

---

1 Julian of Norwich, *Revelations of Divine Love*, trans. Elizabeth Spearing, Penguin Classics, Harmondsworth: Penguin, 1998, p. 7, Third Showing.

Much of this learning and reflecting was not conducted through overtly theological conversation, or even through words at all, but through embodied communal and individual action – making pom-poms – out of which conversation and questions gently flowed.

You can follow up some of these themes in:

Chapter 4: Engaging through the senses

Chapter 12: Medium and message, process and product

Chapter 22: Resources.

22

Resources

Engaging with creation

> '... strive to safeguard the integrity of creation, and sustain
> and renew the life of the earth.'
>> From the Anglican Five Marks of Mission[1]

Possibly the most pressing issue facing the contemporary world (and
there are certainly plenty of issues!) is the way that the human race
is destroying the very environment that sustains us. We are running
out of oil, while being unable to dispose safely of the plastics that
we make from it. We consume more and more, ravaging the planet's
finite resources, and are seemingly unable to co-ordinate a genuinely
global decision to turn things around. New technologies may contribute to solving the problems, but most commentators are agreed
that something far more difficult is needed: a change in attitude
towards the material world.

This is an issue that affects everything, so it must be something
that we think about in relation to our faith. It's certainly something
that we need to be thinking about as we prepare to preach with all
ages. Here are some of the dimensions that might shape our thinking:

---

1 www.anglicancommunion.org/mission/marks-of-mission.aspx.

1 How might we raise some of these issues in the *content* of our preaching? Look through upcoming lectionary readings for opportunities for exploring creation, sustainability, care for the planet and respect for living things and one another.

2 How might we engage differently with our environment as we preach? Preaching might respond more to the natural world: the rhythm of the seasons, the changing length of the days, the growth and decay of the vegetation, even the patterns of the stars and planets.

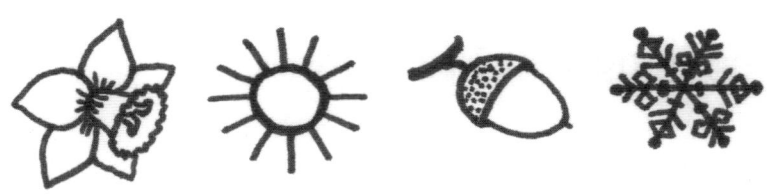

3 How does our relationship with creation affect our thinking as we plan a talk? Try sitting outside or going for a walk while reading through and thinking about the readings. Pay attention to the sights, smells and sounds. Different sensory data leads to different emotional responses and different thought processes.

4 Are there opportunities to go outside, or to bring something from the outside into church for the service? Find out about Wild Church or Forest Church – and visit one if there is one locally – to experience how a church can intentionally inhabit a natural environment so that it is forming their thinking and praying and action.

5 How might our preaching enable people to interact more with the natural world? We can borrow natural objects as resources for our preaching, whether or not the theme is explicitly environmental. Stones, leaves, driftwood or fallen twigs and branches and many more items can all be used to create temporary art, to learn practices of quality attention-paying or to experience wonder. They can then be put back where they came from afterwards.

6 How might the materials we use during all-age preaching reflect our care and concern? Fewer single-use items, especially those that can't be recycled or composted, and fewer plastic items, especially if they can't be reused, is a great start. If something is going to be created during a service, what will happen to  it afterwards, and how it might be disposed of once we no longer need it, may affect the materials we choose to use. This is another area where it's useful to think more widely than preaching: would your church support the idea of an eco-audit? Think with your leadership team about who might lead such a task well, how the congregation could be involved, and how you might share your findings.[2]

7 How might we avoid condoning wastefulness in our preaching and worship? We convey by the way that we handle and use material things that there is a sacredness to all of creation, not just the elements that we call 'holy' in church.

> We invited anyone not planning to eat their Christingle orange to leave it in a box by the door. That evening, we shredded the rind and froze it so that we could make marmalade with it later. They're not really the right kind of oranges, so we added extra pectin. It was better than letting them go to waste.

---

2 There is a survey you can use to approach this here: https://ecochurch.arocha.org.uk/. There is a wealth of ideas under the 'resources' tab, and your church can even apply for an Eco Church award.

Engaging with shoestrings

What about all the churches and preachers that don't have any re-sources, or the skill or time to make them, or who have to do everything on a shoestring? It should be possible to preach with all ages without any of the fancy illustrations, activities and visuals that we might be tempted to rely on. In this book I've tried to include a range of different levels – and kinds – of resourcing:

- Using the gifts that people have offered (like Joan making me all those cushions out of scrap fabric, in Chapter 3).
- Using resources scrounged from Scrapstores or salvaged from other uses (like the cardboard in Chapter 7 and the ribbons in Chapter 5).
- Using relatively cheap and readily available materials (like the bubble mixture in Chapter 19 – you can make your own mixture to refill the bottles).
- Drawing on people more than objects (again, the Pentecost breathing exercise in Chapter 19).
- Using 'found objects' specific to the context (such as the stones in Chapter 17).
- Making things myself (like the worn-out bedsheet Mobius strip in Chapter 9, which required a bit of spatial awareness but very little by way of skill!).

Many of the people who undertake children's ministry and all-age preaching regularly do so on a shoestring, donating resources and hesitating to claim expenses. Even if we do reach a point of being able to claim legitimate expenses, there are good reasons why working with shoestrings can be a good thing in itself.

There will come a day when we have to preach unexpectedly, or without any of the props that we might otherwise rely on – we can start practising for that day now! Resources may be finite, but imagination is not. One of the things we seek to do when we preach with all ages is to encourage people's theological imagination, and the first step towards this is for us, as preachers, to let ourselves be more imaginative, working with what we have and treating it as a gift. When people's imaginations are set free, they will also become more adept at seeing God at work in ordinary things and paying attention to the sacred in everyday life. Nice props and resources can contribute to growth in discipleship, but ultimately we grow in faith through encounter with God, creation and one another.

Everything has potential

A key aspect of the improvisation practice that Robert Poynton explores in his book *Do Improvise*[3] is *use everything* – we probably have more resources than we think. As preachers we can learn to treat everything as full of potential.

This is what Jesus did. Someone would ask him about the Kingdom of God, and he'd usually reply by saying, 'The kingdom of God is like …', and then reflect on something very ordinary that sprang to mind, perhaps an object that was right in front of him or a human action that happens every day. This suggests at least two things:

1   Jesus was brilliant at reflecting theologically 'on the hoof' – we can do this too.
2   There is, genuinely, something of the Kingdom of God in ordinary things.

One of the joys of preaching with all ages in the way that I've tried to describe it in this book is that it invites us into a process of learning to see the beauty in the ordinary, the joy in the unexpected, and the sacred in the material. Everything becomes holy ground.

---

3 Robert Poynton, *Do Improvise*, London: The Do Book Company, 2013.

> Say to yourself (out loud if it helps), 'The Kingdom of heaven is like …' and then let your eye fall on something that is in your immediate field of vision. Pick it up, or look at it in more detail. Consider its form and function, its material and design, what it means to you and where you got it from. How would you use that object to explore with someone something of the Kingdom? If you find it difficult at first, try it with different objects until you get the hang of the process.

Once we are comfortable with the idea of being able to reflect theologically on the ordinary things around us, we will be well placed to be able to use them in preaching if we find ourselves caught short and needing something in a hurry, or if we want to use an item that's indigenous to the place where we are preaching.

How might we help people in a congregation to learn to do this, too?

You are your best resource

Our own self, our life, the things we happen to be carrying with us – these are all up for grabs as we try to help people open up God's word.

> 'Don't get hung up on extravagant props – remember, you are the best visual aid.'
>
> *Mary Hawes*

Stories

If we have a story to tell, we can use it to help people connect life experience with the gospel. We might, during the telling of the story, pause for an 'aside' every so often to help people do this: for example, 'Have you ever been up a mountain, a really big one? Try and picture it in your mind,' or, 'Have you ever been so excited about something that you feel like you might burst?' or, 'Think about a time when you just knew that God was with you. What was that like?'

We need to be aware of what kind of story it is. Does it need telling quickly or slowly, dramatically or reflectively? What are the big ideas in the story and how can we bring them out in the way we tell it? The Godly Play scripts are an excellent example of how theology is woven through story.[4]

The congregation also have stories, and paying attention to someone else's story is one of the most powerful ways of affirming that they matter. Sharing stories in preaching allows people to see their own story in the light of God's love and purposes – what a gift!

Imagination

If we have no paper and no pens, we still have the capacity to imagine a picture. Children, in particular, have an incredible capacity for intensely imagining things. Most people can imagine a picture in their minds – but even if they can't, they may well be able to imagine through their other senses (what does the sun feel like? can you smell the flowers?) and through ideas.

Bodies

We, and the people in our congregations, also have bodies – and our minds and bodies are not separate entities but completely integrated. How might we encourage those in our congregations to consider their own selves as a resource for encountering God?

Julian of Norwich's 'revelations of divine love' are highly embodied visions, the most famous of which is the vision of the hazel nut (see Chapter 21). Holding out our empty cupped hands, and imaginatively placing in them something precious, as if our hands were God's

---

4 To find out more about Godly Play, see www.godlyplay.uk.

own hands, holding all of creation, can be a powerful activity for all ages. We don't need a real hazel nut to do this.

Teresa of Avila's famous challenge is an embodied one:

> 'Christ has no body now but yours. No hands, no feet on earth but yours. Yours are the eyes through which he looks compassion on this world. Yours are the feet with which he walks to do good. Yours are the hands through which he blesses all the world. Yours are the hands, yours are the feet, yours are the eyes, you are his body. Christ has no body now on earth but yours.'
>
> *Teresa of Avila*

A crucial aspect in developing discipleship is connecting what happens in church with the rest of life, and realizing that as the Body of Christ on earth we are called to be active in God's world in the building of God's Kingdom, working out what God is doing and joining in.[5] The hands that receive the bread and wine at Communion are the same 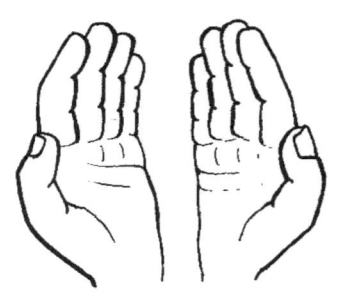 hands that draw or write creatively about God in an interactive talk, the same hands that hold the plate of biscuits and pass it round after the service, and the same hands that continue to bless people Monday to Saturday, in all the contexts in which we find ourselves. If we can make our own embodied selves a key way of opening up God's word, we will take that understanding with us when we leave church, and it will continue to develop and grow during the week.

---

5 Rowan Williams, writing in the Foreword to *Mission Shaped Church*, London: Church House Publishing, 2004.

All-age preaching 'go bag'

In the meantime, it's also worth getting into the habit of looking for ordinary items that we can have in a 'go bag' for all-age preaching, just in case. My 'go bag' included:

- string or ribbon (useful for tying things together, marking out different areas, plaiting, as a washing line to display other items … if you also have clothes pegs!)
- a small bag of stones (though you can pick these up almost any-where, there might be times when you need clean ones in a hurry)
- sticky tape / Blu-tak
- scissors (ideally more than one pair)
- plain stickers (the sort used for printing address labels), for writing names, or the names of characters
- sticky notes (useful for gathering responses anonymously or for display)
- paper (for drawing, writing, making paper aeroplanes or origami shapes, and the 'four corners of God's love'[6])
- pens/pencils.

Adapting your talk

One of the fears that we may have as all-age preachers is that we will arrive expecting an intergenerational congregation and find that there are only adults present. If we've planned a truly all-age talk it should still work, but here are some suggestions to help make sure:

---

6 This is a well-known, easy talk about the way that God's love doesn't run out when we share it – it just grows and grows. Searching for 'corners of God's love' on the internet will lead you to any number of iterations, and it's a great idea to have in your back pocket just in case – all you need is a piece of paper and scissors.

- We can talk before the service with the congregation and find out what they'd like to do. Some adults love engaging with scripture imaginatively and in embodied, creative ways, while others might find this very uncomfortable. Some people may not be as willing or able to move around in the church and do physical activities. If the congregation is very small, one of the big challenges might be getting people to sit near enough to one another to interact. Can we help them feel comfortable about moving closer?
- We can check our 'gospel in the gospel' – is it going to connect with an all-adult congregation? Or can we draw on other ideas we thought about while we were planning?
- If we can't use a planned approach for whatever reason, we may be able to adapt. Could we demonstrate the activity instead? Can we describe it? The congregation might be able to imagine it if it's something they'll have done before (building, plaiting, etc.).
- We needn't be afraid of ending with questions or with more work for the congregation to do. We might encourage them to take the notice sheet home so that they can read the readings again during the week.

But what if the congregation unexpectedly includes several children and we've planned **a** standard adult-friendly sermon?

- It's worth checking whether the children are going to be there when you preach or whether they'll have left to go to their own group.
- Are the children used to hearing adult sermons and quite happy with that?
- Are there minor adjustments we can make to ensure that the children feel included (especially in parts that relate to everyday life – we can make sure any illustrations and examples don't just depend on an adult frame of reference).

If we've prepared an adult-friendly sermon and the congregation is expecting it to be 'all singing all dancing all age' we have a bigger challenge, but there's no need to panic:

- Hopefully we'll have a good idea of the theological and pastoral terrain (see Chapter 2). It's worth taking a moment to recall what the really important points are, and check whether they still feel like they would connect with the congregation we have rather than the one we thought we'd have. (And for next time: even if we're preparing a 'normal'  adults' sermon, it's still worth asking, 'I wonder how I'd do this if it were all age?')
- Can any of the sermon be reframed as conversation, reflection, wondering or imaginative engagement? Open questions can enable both children and adults to engage imaginatively. This is the easiest adaptation, because it doesn't require anything we don't have!
- If we're inviting the congregation to come up with a particular piece of 'applied wisdom', we could invite people to draw their ideas, perhaps doodling them on a blank area of the notice sheet if there's no plain paper, and then talk about their drawings. Younger children, especially, may find it easier to articulate their thoughts through drawing first, and then through speaking about what they have drawn.
- Would anything in the sermon look as if it might resonate with images or objects that people will know, or that are available? It's worth looking round the church for 'found objects', including images in stained-glass windows or on kneelers, and rummaging around for anything useful we happen to have. Remember, everything has potential to help make imaginative connections.
- Changing position or moving to a different part of the church stimulates our senses and makes us more alert. If we have found an object or image to use, can we move to it, or invite children to go

and find it and bring it back? This kind of treasure-hunt approach may help children stay engaged with the process.

What if we've prepared an amazing interactive talk but something goes wrong that stops us doing what we'd planned?

- The projector isn't working ... can we draw our visuals on paper instead, if there's a flipchart around, or invite someone from the congregation who is good at drawing to help? This may end up as an impromptu game of *Pictionary*, in which everyone gets involved, which might be much more actively engaging than a PowerPoint.
- The bag of building bricks is locked in the parish office and nobody has the key ... can we build something out of kneelers or hymn books (carefully and gently), connecting the talk with the place where we are?
- Someone is highly allergic to mustard seeds ... so can we invite people to hold their cupped hands, empty, imagining the tiniest thing they can, holding it carefully and thinking of all its potential?

These look like stumbling blocks, but if we treat them instead as cornerstones they can be a great opportunity to engage the imagination and to draw on the resources around us – everything has potential if we can learn to see it, and the habits we build up through intentionally 'engaging with shoestrings' can help us with this.

23

Reflecting on the dust and the light

I have published elsewhere a talk for use at Christingle services,[1] in which I sprinkle iron powder on the candle flame of the Christingle, to encourage congregations to reflect on what happens when the dull, grey 'dust of the earth' meets the light of Christ – the powder ignites, turning to orange sparks (like a mini sparkler), usually eliciting an 'ooh' from the congregation.

The idea for this talk came when I was with my son (then aged 7) at a science demonstration by Dr Bunhead (from the TV show *Brainiacs*). He blew different metallic powders into a flamethrower to create colourful sparks. It was beautiful and dramatic and really had the 'wow' factor. I knew I wouldn't be able to use a flamethrower in church, but my son and I wanted to find out what would happen just using a candle, so we ordered some iron powder and tested it at home. When we realized that the effect was small but beautiful, we devised the Christingle talk together. He acted as my assistant in the

---

1 Roger Spiller (ed.), *The Canterbury Preachers' Companion 2019*, London: Canterbury Press, 2018, pp. 369–71. The talk was also included in the *Christingle 50* resources published by the Children's Society in 2018.

service (dressed in his lab coat and goggles), holding the Christingle for me while I did the talking and sprinkling.

Having done this talk a few times and reflected on it, several things about it have proved worth noting.

First, while using a flamethrower would have been entertaining (though terrible from a health and safety point of view!) there was something appropriate about what happened being *small*. Christmas is about a world-altering action taking place in a small-scale way – God in the form of a human baby.

Second, the smallness of it meant that when the people nearest to me saw it and responded with their 'ooh!', those further away started craning their necks to see what it was, and went still and quiet in case they missed it. The small scale helped people to pay attention to what was happening, creating a moment of stillness that can be hard to come by in a busy church full of excited children and tired parents.

Third, what is happening with the powder and the flame is a transformation. What is dull and grey becomes bright and shining – something it always had the potential to do. The Children's Society, who began to promote the Christingle in the UK in 1968,[2] work particularly with children and young people who, through abuse, violence, poverty and other issues, might not otherwise reach their potential. The light of Christ shared by the Children's Society not only shines in their darkness, it also enables them to be transformed into people who also shine. Jesus said both 'I am the light of the world' and 'You are the light of the world': using iron powder to reflect on potential realized and transformation of lives connects Jesus' light with our own calling to shine with that same light. We see this reflected in Ireneus, 'The glory of God is a human being fully alive', and Catherine of Siena, 'Be who God meant you to be and you will set the world on fire.'

---

2 The Christingle as a symbol is much older than this, originating in the Moravian Church.

Fourth, I realized that there was something worth reflecting on in the fact that iron is one of the elements not only in the earth but also in us. We are made of the same things as our world – as our universe. The same 118 elements make up the whole of creation, and we are part of that. I've since used the wonderful book *You are Stardust*[3] in conjunction with Christingle in schools to help children explore their relationship with the rest of creation – our responsibility for one another, for our common life and for God's world. The symbol of the Christingle encourages reflection on the world, with all its gifts and needs, and using the iron powder and the flame can help with this process.

Finally, this activity isn't a trick, but depends on real science, and that science is intrinsic to the theological truth being explored. Perhaps this might also help counter the idea from some quarters that we need to choose between faith and science?[4]

---

3 Elin Kelsey, *You are Stardust*, Montreal: Owlkids, 2012 (paperback published 2017).

4 There are many organizations that provide excellent resources to explore this further, such as the Faraday Institute, based in Cambridge.

Encountering God again

Sometimes we are aware that we are curating a moment of wonder and that heaven is touching earth. More often, we only become aware of what God was doing in our preaching later, when we reflect on it or when we start to see its fruits growing in the life of the church. We don't always have to strive for a single 'road to Damascus' experience, but we do need to ask ourselves, 'How is my preaching enabling a real encounter with God?'

The truth is that most of us at some point when we are preaching will forget that God is there. This has happened to me a few times in the process of writing this book. Anxiety (often about whether what we've planned is any good, and whether we'll be able to carry it off) and confidence (as we throw ourselves into the process and see it working) can narrow our focus down to ourselves and the task and leave us in danger of forgetting that God is at the heart of all we are doing.

When we commit to God in prayer all that we think, say and do, from the very moment we start to plan, it is the promptings of the Holy Spirit that guide our preparation; it is the Holy Spirit that empowers our words and actions, and our ability to pay attention to and respond to the unexpected turn, giving us the courage to follow a tangent that we had not thought of, but that has the potential to draw all of us more deeply into an encounter with God; it is the Holy Spirit who gives us wisdom to learn from our experience and gradually shapes us after the pattern of Jesus Christ.

When we look at it like this, preaching (whether we are the preacher or a member of the congregation, and whether or not the context is all age) becomes something that arises from our life with God as well as resourcing it. It is devotional, spiritual, prayerful and bound up with our discipleship as individuals and as communities of faith. This is the approach to preaching that I've aimed to explore in this book.

When we engage with God through our senses we start to bring our whole, embodied selves into God's presence. We learn to discern God's hand in the world around us, and every part of creation becomes something that at any moment might reveal God's love. Our relationship with creation may start to change, as we start to experience every place as holy ground: *God is here.*

When we recognize that God reveals wisdom to infants[1] and is encountered in interruptions and surprises, we will learn to welcome and empower the hidden voices, the difficult question, the insight offered from an unexpected place, and we may find that even the stones start to say, *God is here.*

When we draw deeply on the riches of scripture, theology, liturgy, song and image, we will discover a whole world of encounters with God: stories that have shaped (and are still shaping) the Church and its people. We become part of this tradition as we add to, and hand on to the next generation, what we have received and learned. In our own stories, and the stories we have received from the past, *God is here.*

When we understand better our own preferences and assumptions about worship, prayer and learning, and when we venture out of our comfort zone to try approaching from another direction, we will have encountered God afresh. When we dare to engage with the reality of human experience, weeping with those who weep and rejoicing with those who rejoice, we will find, again, that *God is here.*

When we plan to improvise, charting the terrain and offering a route, but with the courage and humility to listen to others when they show us both hazards and landmarks that would otherwise have passed us by, we will discover that *God is here.*

---

1 Matthew 11.25.

We are all works in progress, pilgrims on a journey. When we dare to take risks, allow ourselves to make mistakes and learn from every experience, we grow in competence and confidence. When we do so prayerfully we will find that trusting ourselves, trusting our congregation and trusting God go hand in hand. Then, in our preaching with all ages, we will find that we are encountering God together.

Further reading and resources

The internet is full of amazing resources, many of them freely offered by fellow practitioners. Sharing our ideas and hearing about how they worked in a different context, as well as developing other people's ideas for our own situation, are great ways for us to learn from one another.

I've found it really useful to share and pool resources in relevant Facebook groups, which have the option of uploading materials in the 'files' section, as well as discussion. I've also enjoyed batting ideas around on Twitter, especially if there's a good, relevant hashtag on the go.

Here are some of the sites that have been most useful to me over the past few years:

www.going4growth.com is the resource hub hosted by the Church of England's National Adviser for Children and Youth. It's a treasure trove of resources from across traditions. From here you can download helpful pieces of research and resource packs, follow links to other useful sites, all arranged thematically, from additional needs to spiritual styles to mission and evangelism. Before you look elsewhere, make sure you've explored this site thoroughly.

http://flamecreativekids.blogspot.co.uk is a searchable blog containing a wealth of devotional activity suggestions, many of which can be adapted for use in all-age worship and in preaching.

www.spiritualchild.co.uk offers resources and articles about children's spirituality and discipleship, including a substantial amount on the value of play.

www.textweek.com is a lectionary-based directory of biblical, liturgical, artistic and cultural resources suitable for service and sermon planning for a range of situations.

www.worshipingwithchildren.blogspot.com is a lectionary-based blog that provides resources for intergenerational worship and learning, as well as articles to resource church leaders more generally in this area.

www.rootsontheweb.com/ is a subscription service, providing lectionary-based materials for children, youth and all age in magazine and online formats.

http://ctm.ucahost.com/CTMR/Growing%20Intergenerational%20Worship.pdf is an excellent resource on developing intergenerational worship.

I have never found it works for me to use someone else's ideas without adapting them, but the following offer some good starting points. There are plenty of others; these are just the ones I have drawn on.

Sandra Millar, *Worship Together: Creating All-Age Services that Work*, London: SPCK, 2012.

Claire Benton Evans, *All-Sorts Worship*, Buxhall: Kevin Mayhew, 2011.

Susan Sayers, *Living Stones* series, Buxhall: Kevin Mayhew.

Sue Wallace, *Multi-Sensory Prayer*, Bletchley: Scripture Union Publishing, 2000.

Wendy Rayner and Annie Slade, *Multi-Sensory Seasons*, Bletchley: Scripture Union Publishing, 2005.

Mina Munns, *We All Share: Introducing Holy Communion to Under 5s through Play, Exploration and Creativity*, Buxhall: Kevin Mayhew, 2018.

Finally, here are a few books that have been extremely useful to me as I have learned to plan and lead worship, and preach, with all ages.

Kate Bruce, *Igniting the Heart: Preaching and the Imagination*, London: SCM Press, 2015.
Although this book isn't about all-age preaching explicitly, the way she talks about creating space around the words is incredibly helpful as a basis for reflective and imaginative engagement with scripture and with God in an all-age context.

Patricia O'Connell Killen and John de Beer, *The Art of Theological Reflection*, New York: Crossroad, 1994.
This offers an approach to theological reflection as an embodied process, engaging with emotion, creativity, symbol and cultural texts. Of all the books on theological reflection, it is probably the most immediately helpful as background reading for preaching with all ages.

Robert Poynton, *Do Improvise*, London: The Do Book Company, 2013.
Drawing on insights and practices from improvisatory theatre, and applying them primarily in the world of business, it contains a surprising amount that is very nearly spirituality and theology.

Be a resource

Most importantly, think about how you can be a resource to yourself and others. Keep a record of what you do – make a note of where an idea came from and how you developed it. If you can, take photographs of both processes and products associated with your all-age preaching (taking care to follow good practice around safeguarding and photography). Record any helpful feedback you get. Keep a note of any real moments of wonder and transformation, journal about the process. Join in discussion locally, and online, in order to share good practice and ideas.

Theme/scripture ....

Place ....

Date/occasion ....

What did I want to happen, and why?	*What actually happened, and why?*
What was better than I hoped?	*What didn't go as well as I hoped?*

What did I learn about myself?	What did I learn about my congregation/context?
What did I learn about God?	**What do I want to add to my 'rummage' drawer?**